Revisioning the Parish Pastoral Council

A Workbook

Mary Ann Gubish and Susan Jenny, S.C., with Arlene McGannon

Illustrated by Mary Kay Neff, S.C.

PAULIST PRESS
New York, N.Y./Mahwah, N.J.

Interior design by Celine M. Allen

Cover design by Tim McKeen

ISBN: 0-8091-3957-X

Published by Paulist Press
997 Macarthur Blvd.
Mahwah, N.J. 07430

www.paulistpress.com

Printed and bound in the United States of America

CONTENTS

PART II: THE SEVEN ESSENTIAL ELEMENTS OF PARISH LIFE

PART III: GUIDE TO PARISH PASTORAL PLANNING

PREFACE

The Church, in response to the ever present inspiration of the Holy Spirit, is continually pouring new wine into new wineskins. This perpetual renewal results from the Spirit's ongoing revelation of Christ's mission for His Church. Revealed both in time and tradition, the revelation of the gospel message for today is the new, robust wine. Hearts open to receive that message are the new wineskins, prepared to carry the wine of God's Word, for Whom the whole world thirsts, into the circumstances of everyday life.

The responsibility of all the baptized in every age is to receive the new wine of God's desire for the Church into fresh, renewed wineskins. By doing so, we build up of the Body of Christ, the Church, in our homes, our parishes, our communities, and our world.

At the parish level, a primary instrument for the flow of this new wine into new wineskins is the parish pastoral council. This leadership body discerns the mission of the parish and envisions the ways in which the parish membership is being called by God to carry out that mission. The parish pastoral council is the vessel through which the new wine is poured into new skins.

REVISIONING THE PARISH PASTORAL COUNCIL presents a new model of ministry for parish pastoral councils. This process has been designed for parishes everywhere in the hope that its implementation will assure the preservation of both the wine of God's desire for us in the Church, and the wineskins of our open response.

This volume is meant to be used as a workbook. It contains factual information, reflection sheets, and sample materials.

> The Prologue presents background information on what a parish pastoral council is, its foundation in the Church's history and tradition, and the movement toward a new model of leadership ministry.
>
> Part I deals with "basics"—prayer, which is the foundation for all council activity, and consensus, the process to be used in council decision-making.
>
> Part II presents a review of the seven essential elements of parish life; these elements provide the framework for the pastoral planning process.
>
> Part III is a guide for the planning process; it explains the components of the pastoral plan, describes the pastoral planning cycle, and offers sugges-

People do not put new wine into old wineskins. Otherwise the skins burst, the wine spills out, and the skins are ruined. Rather, they pour new wine into fresh wineskins, and both are preserved.
—Matthew 9:17

tions for how to go about creating a pastoral plan and for ensuring parish investment in the plan.

Part IV addresses issues relating to the ministry of leadership; it includes material on empowerment, descriptions of roles and responsibilities in the parish and on the council, and practical tips for facilitating meetings and selecting new council members.

The many learning materials and skill development suggestions compiled in this volume are an indication of the complexity of leadership ministry. If a parish pastoral council is to be effective, leadership skills need to be honed. They can guide councils beyond talking about planning to a real and practical visioning and planning process that yields results.

PROLOGUE

A reading from the Gospel of Luke (4:16-21)

Jesus came to Nazareth, where he had grown up, and went according to his custom into the synagogue on the sabbath day. He stood up to read and was handed a scroll of the prophet Isaiah. He unrolled the scroll and found the passage where it was written:

> "The Spirit of the Lord is upon me,
> because he has anointed me
> to bring glad tidings to the poor.
> He has sent me
> to proclaim liberty to captives
> and recovery of sight to the blind,
> to let the oppressed go free,
> and to proclaim a year acceptable to the Lord."

Rolling up the scroll, he handed it back to the attendant and sat down, and the eyes of all in the synagogue looked intently at him. He said to them, "Today this scripture passage is fulfilled in your hearing."

How do you and your parishioners continue to carry out the mission of Christ?

The Parish Pastoral Council

The Second Vatican Council called for the creation of "parish councils." In the Decree on the Apostolate of Lay People, #26, we read:

> In dioceses, as far as possible, councils should be set up to assist the Church's apostolic work, whether in the field of evangelization and sanctification or in the fields of charity, social relations and the rest...
>
> Such councils should be established too, if possible, at parochial, inter-parochial, inter-diocesan level, and also on the national and international planes.[1]

Parish councils were to serve in an advisory capacity to the pastor, and were to utilize the many and varied gifts of the laity in service to the Church as it continues to carry out the mission of Christ.

Over time, while parish councils continued to function in this advisory role, they also became more task-oriented. The parish council model came to include various committees staffed by elected council members who invested a great deal of time and energy in creating and financing programs and making them happen.

Members of councils were usually the "doers" in the parish. Their presence on the council assured the pastor that things would get done, in keeping with the task-orientation that had come to characterize parish councils. As a result, parishes have had many and varied programs, successful festivals and fundraisers, well-maintained facilities, and a variety of social events. The parish council was often the vehicle through which these programs were initiated, received the pastor's approval, obtained the necessary funding, and were implemented.

In recent years, this pattern has shifted toward the creation of "parish pastoral councils." The change, which involves more than simply the addition of a word, has created an entirely new role for these councils. Rather than focusing on specific program planning and implementation, the new model calls for bodies which lead the parish community in the discernment and expression of its mission. This new role presents a challenge to parishes: they must redefine the nature of their leadership and call forth those who are best gifted to serve in that capacity.

The role of the parish pastoral council is, through ongoing pastoral planning, to maintain the integrity of the parish mission and the goals and objectives related to it. Within this new model, programs and events continue to take place in the parish through the efforts of many dedicated parishioners, always in the context of the parish mission and its pastoral plan.

Historical Background

The shift from a practical to a pastoral emphasis for councils is rooted in early church tradition, the relatively recent decrees of the Second Vatican Council, the 1983 revision of the Code of Canon Law, and current developments in individual local churches. A review of each of these will enhance our understanding of the new significance of parish pastoral councils.

The Church in apostolic times was communal in nature. Small groups of Christians formed to support one another through prayer, service, and the distribution of temporal goods. The emphasis was on the many and varied gifts of the members, as well as on each person's responsibility to place those gifts at the service of the community.

> The community of believers was of one heart and mind, and no one claimed that any of his possessions was his own, but they had everything in common. With great power the apostles bore witness to the resurrection of the Lord Jesus, and great favor was accorded them all. There was no needy person among them, for those who owned property or houses would sell them, bring the proceeds of the sale, and put them at the feet of the apostles, and they were distributed to each according to need. (Acts 4:32-35)

> As each one has received a gift, use it to serve one another as good stewards of God's varied grace. Whoever preaches, let it be with the words of God; whoever serves, let it be with the strength that God supplies, so that in all things God may be glorified through Jesus Christ, to whom belong glory and dominion forever and ever. Amen. (1 Peter 4:10-11)

In the late apostolic and early post-apostolic era, the need for more structure arose among these communities of believers. Leadership roles that emerged were filled by presbyters and deacons, who had been chosen by the Lord from among the people. Because of the particular gifts and talents these individuals possessed, the community affirmed them as leaders. All other baptized members continued to discern ways in which they could best follow the gospel message of charity and justice.

The fourth and fifth centuries saw the development of what we now know as parishes and pastors. Although new forms and functions were developing (particularly as the result of the First Council of Nicea in 325), the parish was still very much the localized community of believers, all of whom took responsibility for the mission of the local church according to their various roles.

The model started to shift in the sixth and seventh centuries when bishops began appointing pastors and establishing accompanying pastoral duties and responsibilities. This gradual movement toward a distinction between clergy and a laity was to change the course of church leadership into our own time. By the eighth and ninth centuries, pastors' authority over parishes became more absolute and increasingly well-defined. As heresies continued to arise and to threaten the integrity of the Church, the need for more definitive doctrine and dogma became clearer and again set the tone for the way in which local communities were to be structured and directed for centuries to come.

The Middle Ages brought a widening chasm between clergy and laity. Monasteries arose and became focal points for worship and spiritual life. It was also within the monasteries that most education took place, thereby restricting the pool of power and leadership in both society and the Church.

The significance of the parish as the locus for experiencing and living out one's faith dwindled. Although parishes came to be defined as territorial (by the Council of Trent, 1545–63), the loyalty of the faithful was not so clearly delineated. The loyalties of many could be found with a particular monastery or movement more than with a geographically bounded parish.

During this period, the priesthood was further defined in terms of eligibility requirements, lifestyle elements, allegiance to the bishop, and role within parishes, particularly as pastor. As this role became increasingly strengthened, the role of the laity conversely declined. Both the pastoral and practical leadership of the parish now rested solely with the pastor. This diminished involvement of the laity in the leadership and life of the Church was to remain the norm for centuries, until the Second Vatican Council.

VATICAN II

The Second Vatican Council was announced by Pope John XXIII on January 25, 1959, and the first session was held nearly four years later on October 11, 1962. Three years of meetings followed, ending on December 8, 1965.

The Council issued sixteen documents including the Dogmatic Constitution on the Church (*Lumen Gentium*) in 1964, the Pastoral Constitution on the Church in the Modern World (*Gaudium et Spes*) in 1965, and the Decree on the Apostolate of the Laity (*Apostolicam Actuositatem*) in 1965. Through these and the post-conciliar documents that followed, the bishops turned the tide of Catholicism and brought the Church into the modern era.

"Ever since the Second Vatican Council, the Church has been sifting through a burst of theological reflection on its own nature and identity."[2] Much of that reflection has been focused upon the appropriate roles of the clergy and laity in the life of the Church. From its definition of the Church as "the People of God"[3] to the opening words of the Decree on the Apostolate of the Laity: "In its desire to intensify the apostolic activity of the People of God, the Council now earnestly turns its thoughts to the Christian laity,"[4] the Council sought to empower the baptized to claim their critical role in bringing about the Kingdom of God.

Repeatedly, the bishops revived the reality of the early Church as a community of faith where all the baptized bear responsibility for placing their individual gifts at the service of all. This service takes place primarily at the parish level where the faithful gather together in prayer, work together to create community, and live the Gospel in the midst of everyday life.

> Participators in the function of Christ, priest, prophet, and king, the laity have an active part of their own in the life and action of the Church. Their action within the Church communities is so necessary that without it the apostolate of the pastors will frequently be unable to obtain its full effect.[5]

Clergy and laity who receive the wine of the gospel message into fresh wineskins enable the existence and the effectiveness of the Church's mission in the world. Without an active laity, living out their baptismal call to holiness and service, the ministry of the clergy is diminished and ultimately ineffectual. The laity breathe life into the gospel message preached by the clergy and celebrated with them in the sacraments. Without a significant degree of mutual support among clergy and laity, both the wine and wineskins could be lost.

Vatican II emphasized this crucial role of the laity time and time again:

Inserted as they are in the Mystical Body of Christ by baptism and strengthened by the power of the Holy Spirit in confirmation, it is by the Lord himself that they are assigned to the apostolate.[6]

The laity accomplish the Church's mission in the world principally by that blending of conduct and faith which makes them the light of the world.[7]

This renaissance of the role of all the baptized in the Church led to multiple levels of increased lay involvement in parish life: as liturgical ministers in a variety of capacities, as financial advisors, as catechists and teachers, as active participants in social ministry, and in a variety of other ways. Many of the laity rose to the scriptural challenge put before them by the Second Vatican Council:

As each one has received a gift, use it to serve one another as good stewards of God's varied grace. (1 Peter 4:10)

The creation of parish councils by Vatican II provided yet another way in which lay persons could serve the local church. Their role as members of the parish council was principally a practical one, advising the pastor on fiscal matters and planning various parish events. The concept of a leadership body which could discern and articulate the pastoral mission of the parish had not yet evolved. Nevertheless, participation in these early councils was often the first real instance of lay involvement in decisions about parish life.

As noted in a translation of the council documents published shortly after the conclusion of Vatican II,

The renewal of the Church, called for by the documents of the Council, depends in great part on a laity that fully understands not only these documents, but also their co-responsibility for the mission of Christ in the world.[8]

The clergy, for their part, were to welcome, encourage, enable, and inspire the laity to carry out this shared responsibility.

1983 CODE OF CANON LAW

To reflect the exciting, ongoing movement of the Holy Spirit in the Church, Pope John XXIII called for a revision of the 1917 Code of Canon Law. The revised code was promulgated in 1983 by Pope John Paul II. Echoing the spirit of Vatican II, the new code emphasized the collegial nature of the Church. This is particularly evident in the code's definition of a parish:

> A parish is a definite community of the Christian faithful established on a stable basis within a particular church [diocese]; the pastoral care of the parish is entrusted to a pastor as its own shepherd under the authority of the diocesan bishop. (Canon 515, §1)[9]

The canons also define the role of the laity in the local church:

> The Christian faithful are those who, inasmuch as they have been incorporated into Christ through baptism, have been constituted as the people of God; for this reason, since they have become sharers in Christ's priestly, prophetic and royal office in their own manner, they are called to exercise the mission which God has entrusted to the Church to fulfill in the world, in accord with the condition proper to each one. (Canon 204)

and call for the establishment of parish pastoral councils:

> After the diocesan bishop has listened to the presbyteral council and if he judges it opportune, a pastoral council is to be established in each parish; the pastor presides over it, and through it the Christian faithful along with those who share in the pastoral care of the parish in virtue of their office give their help in fostering pastoral activity. (Canon 536, §1)

By virtue of their baptism, then, the laity are empowered to participate in the mission of the Church and in the "pastoral activity" of the parish, a community of believers striving to experience more fully the Kingdom of God in a particular time and place. One of the ways in which the laity can exercise that call is through the ministry of the parish pastoral council.

Toward a New Model

Even prior to Vatican II, certain parishes had set up church committees to serve in an advisory capacity to the pastor. These committees were primarily responsible for the oversight of parish programmatic and fiscal concerns.

After Vatican II, these committees gradually evolved into parish councils. The goal of REVISIONING THE PARISH PASTORAL COUNCIL is to assist parishes in moving from the current parish council model to that of the parish pastoral council, as called for in the revised Code of Canon Law. The following diagram illustrates this movement:

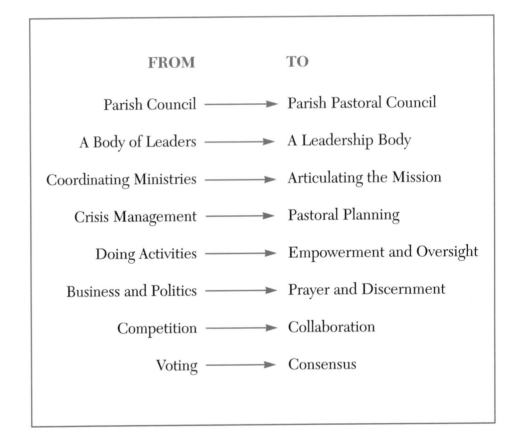

FROM		TO
Parish Council	→	Parish Pastoral Council
A Body of Leaders	→	A Leadership Body
Coordinating Ministries	→	Articulating the Mission
Crisis Management	→	Pastoral Planning
Doing Activities	→	Empowerment and Oversight
Business and Politics	→	Prayer and Discernment
Competition	→	Collaboration
Voting	→	Consensus

In order to make a successful transition from the parish council model to the pastoral council model, it is necessary to lay the groundwork in terms of mission and vision.

Mission and Vision

The purpose of revisioning the council is primarily the development of mission-focused parishes, rather than programmatic or finance-driven ones. This, of course, does not deny the importance of activity and fiscal responsibility in a parish. It does attempt to place at the heart of the parish a consciousness of and zeal for the mission of Jesus Christ. When there is a clear awareness of this "larger vision" proposed by the gospels and taught by the Church, a parish finds itself energized by a sense of mission and directed to matters that will do more than simply fill the annual calendar.

Jesus, early in his ministry, proclaimed what his mission on earth was. Through the generations, Christians have attempted to express that mission in concrete ways. The mission of the diocese and the mission of the parish are shaped by the Church's two-thousand-year tradition and ultimately grounded in the mission of Christ.

THE THEOLOGY OF MISSION

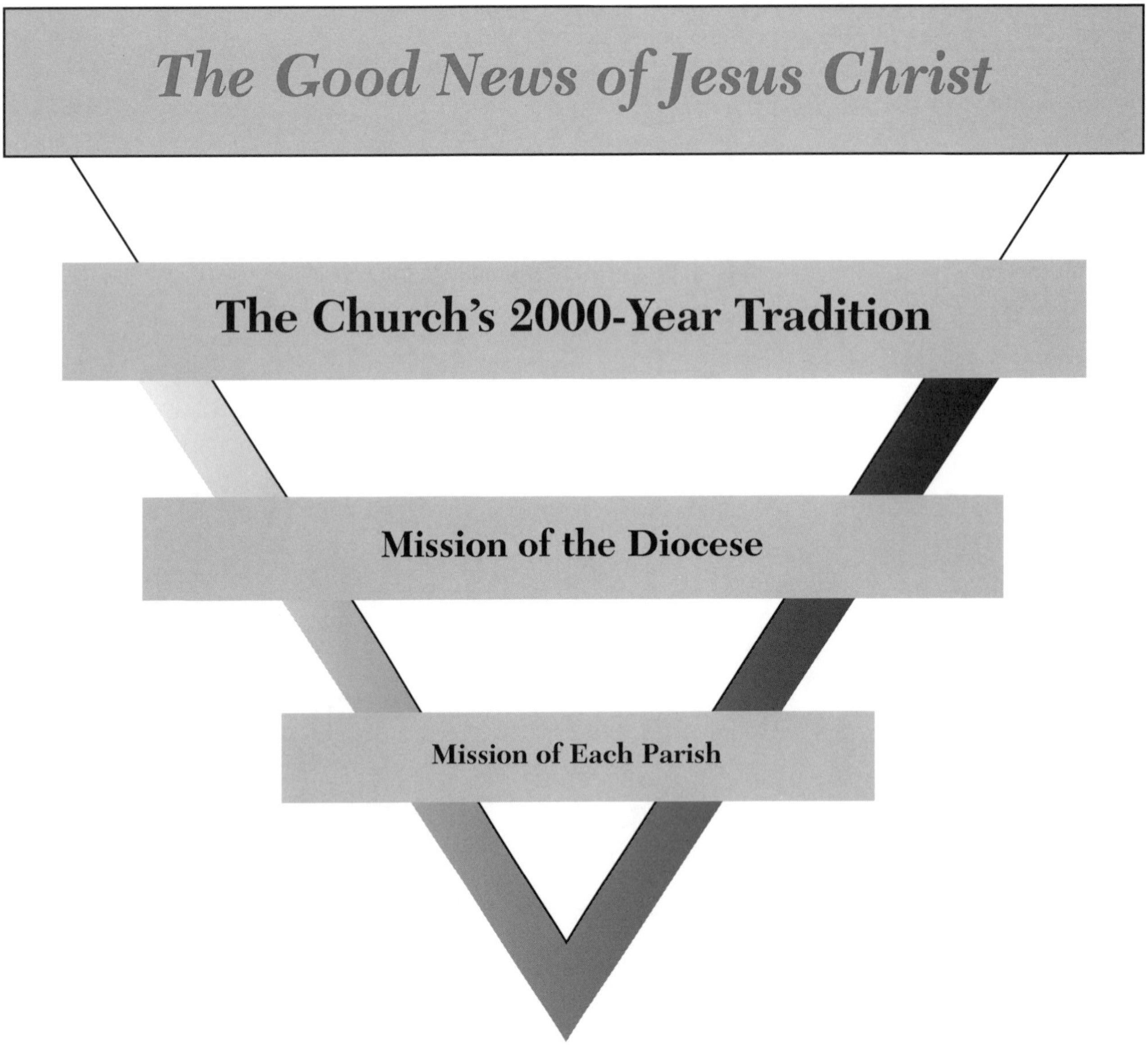

THE MISSION OF THE DIOCESE

Many dioceses have adopted mission statements. These statements summarize the identity, call, and responding action of the People of God in the local church. They also give direction and shape to the diocesan response to the call of God. For example:

Sample Diocesan Mission Statement

We, the people of this Catholic diocese, believe that we have been called by God to be the church of Jesus Christ in the rural, urban, and resort communities of this area. Commissioned to proclaim the Good News of Jesus Christ in worship and service, we find our strength in the sacraments of initiation, especially within the unity of a eucharistic community. We continue the mission of Jesus in our ministry, empowered by the Holy Spirit and guided by the pastoral leadership of our bishop.

We intend to be stewards of the persons, races, and cultures which are our greatest assets, as well as of the material and spiritual resources entrusted to us. We pledge to challenge and to encourage individuals, families, parishes and the community at large to make their faith journeys toward the Kingdom of God.

We accept our obligation to reflect upon church and societal issues and to use our gifts and resources to practice gospel justice, to heal divisive wounds among God's people, and to join with all people of good will in acting to alleviate human suffering.

To bring this vision to reality, we will plan strategically, develop goals and objectives, and invite persons across the diocese to join in action for the glory of God and in service to the mission of this local church.

Looking at a Diocesan Mission Statement

Part I: Review the above mission statement and take time to jot down what you think each of these phrases means. Then discuss with others around the table the meanings they found. If there are phrases that all are unsure about, take time to do some research and bring back to the group what you have discovered and any new insights you may have come to.

The Good News of Jesus Christ ______________________________

Sacraments of initiation ______________________________

Eucharistic community ______________________________

The mission of Jesus ______________________________

Ministry ______________________________

Pastoral ______________________________

Stewards ______________________________

Faith journeys ______________________________

Kingdom of God ______________________________

Gospel justice ______________________________

All people of good will ______________________________

Plan strategically ______________________________

Glory of God ______________________________

Local church ______________________________

Part II. Now, if your diocese has a mission statement, break open the words of that statement in an exercise similar to this one. Allow time for participants to jot down their understanding of the highlighted phrases and terms. Then discuss the meaning and implications of these words for the mission of your diocese and your parish.

THE MISSION OF THE PARISH

"The parish is where the Church lives. Parishes are communities of faith, of action, and of hope. They are where the Gospel is proclaimed and celebrated, where believers are formed and sent to renew the earth."[10] In addition to one's family of origin, the parish is the place where a person first experiences a community of faith and where one is formed and sustained in that faith.

Each parish, as a "definite community of the Christian faithful" (Canon 515), has a unique mission. The essential mission of every parish is evangelization, proclaiming and witnessing to the Good News of the Gospel by enacting Jesus' command: "Go, therefore, and make disciples of all nations, baptizing them in the name of the Father, and of the Son, and of the holy Spirit" (Matt 28:19).

Just as a diocese needs to articulate the universal mission of the Church in ways specific to the local church, so too must each parish discern and articulate the gospel call in its own way. Every parish mission should flow from and be a unique expression of the diocesan vision.

The specific mission of a parish, articulated in the parish mission statement, is determined by the gifts and charisms of the local church, the needs of the People of God, and the means by which the community can respond to those needs.

The parish mission, then, is the unique and particular way in which a parish places its gifts at the service of the local and the universal Church.

I: BASICS

PRAYER

THE IMPORTANCE OF COUNCIL PRAYER AND REFLECTION

The parish is a community of people who believe in Jesus, who listen to the "Good News" and try to live it out, and who celebrate and pray together. Clergy and council form a microcosm of the parish community of faith. Hence, as parish leaders, they must be about the task of continual renewal—growth in their faith journeys throughout life. Members of the parish pastoral council need to have opportunities to pray with one another in order to deepen their individual and communal holiness.

Prayer helps Christians experience the value and joy of communion both with God and with other members of the People of God. It is also a source for personal and communal integration. To become stronger in their prayer life, here are some questions individual council members might consider:

What is prayer?

When and how do I pray?

What does prayer mean to me?

How can prayer make me a more whole (holy) person?

How does prayer link me to my parish community?

Council members are encouraged to discuss these questions and also consider the ways in which prayer and reflection can animate each council meeting. The council is strongly encouraged to set aside at least fifteen minutes of each session for prayer. Nothing should deter the group from spending this precious time well. They may also join together for an annual retreat and/or periodic days of reflection as a means of strengthening the bonds of faith which bind them together and, in turn, to the parish and the total Church.

While certain members of the group (the spiritual formation team) will have responsibility for structuring council prayer, every member is integral to the prayer of the group. Personal preparation for the meeting, a certain eagerness for sharing matters of the spirit, and full attention and participation are every member's responsibility.

Naturally, the scriptures may shape a council's prayer, but just as valid would be the use of a church document or a pertinent article. Oftentimes, prayer can lead to or flow from a study session on a topic of some relevance to the council.

There are other times when praying the Liturgy of the Hours—for example, Evening Prayer—may be appropriate. Occasionally, when the opportunity presents itself, councils may wish to gather together at Eucharist. Even in these more formal situations, every effort should be made to allow for some faith sharing, a homily open to participative reflection, and/or intercessory prayers from the group.

No matter how they pray, the important thing is that councils make the time and actually do it. Not only is this a source of strength and guidance for the ministry of leadership, but it forms the council into a community of faith at the heart of the parish. And that is what makes all the difference.

1. Choose a Theme

- The theme is not a random selection. It is determined by any number of factors that are part of the everyday life and experience of the parish and the council.
- Look at the agenda. Perhaps there is an important decision coming up. Perhaps a discussion on a particular goal will occur. The theme of the prayer will then reflect the major topic of the agenda.
- Use a seasonal theme, e.g., Advent, Pentecost, the fall harvest, summertime, etc.
- Select a developmental/growth theme, a topic that will help the group to develop as a faith community, e.g., listening, commitment, healing, etc.
- Use the daily readings or a Sunday reading close to the date of the meeting. There is always a way to link themes from the regular readings into the parish's life story.
- Be especially attentive to the "big picture" in the area. Have there been major disruptions in the community, such as a devastating storm, the closing of a local industry that has resulted in unemployment, an accidental or violent death that has shaken the parish community, a transition in the pastor/pastoral staff? Themes of death/resurrection, loss and grief, community outreach may suggest themselves naturally.

2. Develop the Prayer Experience

Suggested here is one simple format that could be used. It should take about half an hour. As the group gains experience and confidence in planning for prayer, other creative alternatives may emerge.

- *Call to Prayer.* Use a song, a simple greeting and response, an invitation to silence and some quiet time.
- *Scripture Reading.* Choose a short passage which highlights your theme. A Concordance may help locate appropriate texts. The leader may give a short commentary elaborating on the context or background of the passage. Most recent editions of the Bible have sufficient notes to help even an inexperienced leader.
- *Response to the Reading.* Use a song, a psalm, silence, soft music. This period of the prayer should take at least five minutes to allow time for reflection.

- *Sharing Our Experiences.* Prepare carefully one or two questions which invite the participants to relate the reading to their own lives and the life of the parish. These questions may be posed as part of the silent "response" period or they may be posed when it ends. Ask participants to share in groups of two or three or, if the group is not too large, with everyone. Allow between fifteen and twenty minutes for this. Draw all the responses together at the end of this time period.

- *Praying for Our Needs.* Invite the group to mention personal or parish concerns for which the group will pray. Use a standard intercessory prayer form, with a response such as, "Lord, hear our prayer."

- *Call to Work.* Use a song, a refrain, a blessing which will extend the prayer into the work which will be done. This can serve as a transition into the business of the meeting.

3. Prepare the Setting

- Prayer can take place where the meeting will be held or in a different space. Both have their merits. Remember: environment is very important. Sometimes praying around a cluttered worktable can be a way of offering the work to God. However, if the work is a distraction, the table should be cleared off.

- The setting for prayer provides a place where participants can be comfortable and at ease. A quiet, warm, and inviting atmosphere helps bring the Spirit into the persons and the space where they gather. The room should be neither too hot nor too cold, neither too large nor too small, neither drafty nor stuffy. Chairs should not be so comfortable as to put people to sleep, nor so hard as to create physical discomfort. Light should be neither blinding nor too faint. Circular seating is helpful for prayer, so that when time comes for reflective conversation all may see and attend to one another.

- Music or a simple centerpiece with candle, Bible, or other sacred symbol helps as well. The use of incense, water, light or anything that touches the senses can create a sense of the holy in the midst of a quite ordinary setting.

- Generally walk through the prayer before you begin to pray, so that all the needed directions are given ahead of time. Be sure that all who will have particular responsibilities during the prayer time know exactly what they are to do and when. This allows you to maintain a reflective tone throughout the prayer.

- Be sure that all materials are available: song books, prayer sheets, other elements of the prayer service. When using a tape recorder or other equipment, be sure to test it ahead of time, rather than discovering problems during the prayer.

Remember a few other details:

- Although prayer can occur at any time during the meeting, using it to start is preferred. If you pray at the end of the meeting, be sure to allow sufficient time. If the meeting runs longer than anticipated, prayer tends to be rushed or shortened.

- Silence is a very important part of prayer, not only to listen to the voice of God, but also to allow the Spirit time to work in everyone. Taking time at the beginning for just "quieting down" will allow people to clear their minds and hearts of all the other details of their busy lives, and to bring their attention fully to the Lord.

- Prayer is the heart of the work of the pastoral council. Try to keep the spirit of prayer throughout the meeting. At times it will be helpful to stop the process to recall the Lord's presence, or a word or phrase from the prayer, or to ask for wisdom and guidance. It should be as natural as pausing to take a breath.

Planning Prayer for Pastoral Council Meetings

Meeting Date ______________________________

Theme ______________________________

Setting and Environment (*Check off or circle any details which need to be arranged.*)

_____ Furniture arrangement
_____ Sacred objects (water, candle, Bible, picture, incense, other related object)
_____ Equipment (tape or CD player, VCR and TV)
_____ Materials (hymn books, prayer pages, scriptures, other texts for reflection)
_____ Heating and lighting adjustments

Call to Prayer (*Check off or write in selections.*)

_____ Silence
_____ Sung hymn
_____ Taped song or soft music
_____ Invitation from prayer leader
_____ Gesture, such as sign of the cross, use of holy water

Opening Prayer (*Check off choice; if it is to be read, select or prepare it.*)

_____ Spontaneous at the discretion of prayer leader _____ Selected or prepared prayer

Scriptures or Other Reading (*Note text here.*) ______________________________

Response to Reading (*Check off or write in selections.*)

_____ Silence _____ Sung hymn
_____ Psalm _____ Taped song or soft music

Reflection Question(s) (*Plan these very carefully and write them down.*)

____

____

Intercessory Prayer (*Check off choice; if prepared petitions are to be used, get them ready.*)

_____ Totally spontaneous petitions
_____ Some prepared petitions to begin intercessions
_____ Response
_____ Our Father (traditional ending to intercessory prayer)

Conclusion or Transition to Meeting (*Make choice and prepare it.*)

_____ Song
_____ Blessing
_____ Other

Checklist: Parish Pastoral Council Prayer and Reflection

This exercise is helpful at the beginning of each new year or perhaps during the annual retreat day. It is suggested that each member complete the checklist individually, and then that the group discuss the results with the aim of improving the quality of their prayer and reflection in the future.

_____ Members of the council's spiritual formation team prepare and lead prayer, involving other council members in the prayer and reflection.

_____ Our prayer helps us make the transition from daily chatter to the work of council.

_____ Our prayer is integral to the agenda and deliberations of the council.

_____ Our prayer usually takes at least fifteen minutes.

_____ We allow some time in our prayer for people to mention their intentions and pray for the needs of the parish.

_____ We pray in a pattern like the Liturgy of the Word, with song, prayer, readings, reflection, and petitions.

_____ We pray in various ways, but always include some use of scripture or church documents, allowing time for silence and for spoken reflection on the selected text.

_____ We pray to open our meetings.

_____ We pray when we are struggling with an issue or doing discernment.

_____ I pray personally to deepen my own awareness of God's role in my life.

_____ I pray personally for my pastor and other council members.

_____ I pray personally for the good of our parish community.

_____ I pray personally for the sick, the suffering, the needy, and the neglected of our parish.

_____ I pray personally for our diocese and for the Church throughout the world.

_____ Our pastoral council has a broad study plan relating to the "seven essential elements of parish life" and we set aside time in every meeting for learning together.

_____ We subscribe to a few good publications on parish life and use them for discussion of our own parish and its life and growth.

_____ We occasionally watch a video or invite a speaker on a topic of interest to our council.

CELEBRATING THE MINISTRY OF LEADERSHIP

Invitation to Prayer

Leader: The grace of our Lord Jesus Christ and the fellowship of the Holy Spirit be with us during this meeting

All: To strengthen and guide us in all our undertakings.

Opening Prayer

Leader: Let us pray:
Lord Jesus, by your example you taught us to serve one another without counting the cost. Your Kingdom is not one of this world, but rather one where those who are greatest must think of themselves as the least. Your leadership did not seek power and acclaim. Rather, your authority was gentle, persuasive, and pastoral. Inspire us for the ministry of leadership in our parish, that we might put your people's needs ahead of our own and direct every decision and action to the fulfillment of your mission here on earth. We pray this in your name, Jesus Christ, one God with the Father and the Spirit, forever and ever.

All: Amen.

Reading

Reader: A reading from the first letter of Peter (1 Pt 5:1-4)

So I exhort the presbyters among you, as a fellow presbyter and witness to the sufferings of Christ and one who has a share in the glory to be revealed. Tend the flock of God in your midst, overseeing not by constraint but willingly, as God would have it, not for shameful profit but eagerly. Do not lord it over those assigned to you, but be examples to the flock. And when the chief Shepherd is revealed, you will receive the unfading crown of glory.

The Word of the Lord.

All: Thanks be to God.

Reflection

After a few minutes of silence to consider the message of these words addressed to pastoral leaders, share responses to these questions:

- What obligation do we as a council have to be an "example to the flock?"

- What challenges do we face in being that example, either individually or as a council?

- What areas of our faith-in-action are especially important to our witness as leaders?

Intercessions

Leader: Let us gather our prayers now for the needs of the parish and especially this evening for ourselves as council members. Our response will be: Make us leaders, true servants of your flock.

– Enkindle a deep desire in us for spiritual growth in our lives and in the life of our parish, we pray

– Give us an infectious enthusiasm for the future of our parish, we pray

– Grant us wisdom as we gather our parishioners to make decisions about parish directions, we pray

– Unite us as we seek consensus on what you desire for our parish, we pray

– Teach us trust and openness to your truth as we speak and listen to one another, we pray

– Help us stimulate the generosity of your people by empowering them to assume responsibility for the tasks to which you call this community, we pray

– Bestow on us your creative Spirit and flexibility in our work with people and ideas, that your mission be accomplished in our midst, we pray

Here, add intentions for the present needs of the world, the parish, parishioners, council members.

Leader: Let us pray, united as brothers and sisters, in the name of Jesus and as he taught us: Our Father...
Now let us move into the work for which we have gathered. May God—the creative Father, + the compassionate Son, and the inspiring Spirit—bless us in all we do at this meeting.

All: Amen.

At the conclusion of the meeting, the council may pray as follows:

Leader: We thank you, Jesus, our servant leader and true shepherd, that you have called us to share the ministry of leadership.

All: We rejoice that you have entrusted to each one of us
gifts and talents for the service of this parish and your Church.

We thank you for your confidence in us despite our limitations,
and ask that you make up for what is lacking in our sincere efforts.

Help us discover your purpose and direction for our parish community, and keep us always mindful of the mission you have set before us.

Teach us to be leaders after your own heart. Let us look with your eyes, hear with your ears, walk in your steps and decide according to your will. Help us stand in the midst of your people as examples the whole flock can follow.

We praise and bless you with gratitude for the gift of baptism
and the call to mission in service of your Church and the world.
We thank you, Jesus, our servant leader and true shepherd,
that you have called us to share the ministry of leadership.

Amen.

ON THE VALUE OF PRAYER

Invitation to Prayer

Leader: We gather in the divine presence and ask that our prayer be pleasing to God.

All: May our prayer rise up like incense, our hands outstretched like an evening offering.

Leader: In the name of the Father, + and of the Son and of the Holy Spirit.

All: Amen

Opening Hymn

Select a hymn of praise and gratitude, such as:

This Day God Gives Me
Baptized in Water
I Come with Joy
All People Who on Earth Do Dwell
All Creatures of Our God and King
Let All Things Now Living

Opening Prayer

Leader: Let us pray.
Lord Jesus, you are our teacher, you are our example. In you, we have become disciples. Strengthen us for the task you set before us, nothing less than continuing your mission here on earth. Help us to know that mission and to embrace it with selflessness and tireless enthusiasm. Be with us in all our efforts to live out and to pass on your Gospel. We pray this in your name, Jesus Christ, who with the Father and the Holy Spirit are one God, forever and ever. Amen.

Reading

Reader: A reading from the Gospel according to Mark (Mark 1:32-39)

When it was evening, after sunset, they brought to him all who were ill or possessed by demons. The whole town was gathered at the door. He cured many who were sick with various diseases, and he drove out many demons, not permitting them to speak because they knew him.

Rising very early before dawn, he left and went off to a deserted place, where he prayed. Simon and those who were with him pursued him and on finding him said, "Everyone is looking for you." He told them, "Let us go on to the nearby villages that I may preach there also. For this purpose have I come." So he went into their synagogues, preaching and driving out demons throughout the whole of Galilee.

The Gospel of the Lord.

All: Praise to you, Lord Jesus Christ.

Reflection

- How do you suppose Jesus had the energy to continue his mission, especially when "the whole town was gathered at the door" and everybody was looking for him?

- What does the example of Jesus living out the "purpose" for which he had come say to you as a pastoral council member?

Allow these reflections to move the council into its agenda. At the conclusion of the meeting, spontaneous intercessions may be made for the needs of the parish.

FOR A PASTORAL MISSION

Invitation to Prayer

Leader: Where two or more of you are gathered,

All: There I am in your midst.

Leader: Be with us, Lord Jesus, for we gather in your name.

All: Come, Lord Jesus, come!

Opening Hymn

Select a hymn on mission or ministry, such as:

Lord, You Give the Great Commission
Lord, Whose Love in Humble Service
We Are Your People
As a Fire Is Meant for Burning
Be Not Afraid
We Are Called
Song of the Body of Christ
You Have Anointed Me

Reading

Reader: A reading from the Gospel of Luke (Luke 4:16-21)

Jesus came to Nazareth, where he had grown up, and went according to his custom into the synagogue on the sabbath day. He stood up to read and was handed a scroll of the prophet Isaiah. He unrolled the scroll and found the passage where it was written:

"The Spirit of the Lord is upon me,
because he has anointed me
to bring glad tidings to the poor.
He has sent me to proclaim liberty to captives
and recovery of sight to the blind,
to let the oppressed go free,
and to proclaim a year acceptable to the Lord."

Rolling up the scroll, he handed it back to the attendant and sat down, and the eyes of all in the synagogue looked intently at him. He said to them, "Today this scripture passage is fulfilled in your hearing."

The Gospel of the Lord.

All: Praise to you, Lord Jesus Christ.

Reflection

Just as Jesus was able to proclaim that he fulfilled the words of Isaiah the prophet, so too must we as a parish be able to proclaim that we fulfill the words of Jesus. How are the words we just read fulfilled in our parish?

After sharing faith, the council may proceed to its agenda. The litany that follows may be used to conclude the opening prayer or the council meeting itself.

Litany for a Pastoral Mission

Leader: Let us now bring to the Lord Jesus, who challenges us to fulfill his mission, our prayers that we might be his ministers today. As we invoke the Spirit, let us pray...

All: Empower us, Lord, for the work of ministry.

Leader: For a true spirit of worship in our parish, that our Sunday Eucharist might both celebrate and express our faith as a community gathered, we pray...

For the spirit of evangelization in our parish, that in all we do we might proclaim the Good News of the Kingdom of God, we pray...

For a spirit of unselfish Christian service, that our actions on behalf of others may reach beyond our own concerns, we pray...

For the powerful spirit of your Word, that in our formation efforts all persons may find truth, guidance, and challenge on their lifelong journeys of faith, we pray...

For the enlivening spirit of a faith-filled community, that our parish may be a dynamic witness to unity and compassion in this area, we pray...

For a generous spirit of stewardship, that the gifts and talents of all our people may be directed to the building up of a shared responsibility for the Church's mission, we pray...

For the spirit of leadership, that courageous and visionary collaboration may help shape the life of this community and our local church, we pray...

Let us pray now with the words given to us by Jesus, in whose name all our ministry finds its source: Our Father... for the Kingdom and the power and the glory are yours, now and forever. Amen.

Leader: Stay with us Lord, as we continue to work in your name,

All: Bless us + and keep us and let your face shine upon us. Amen.

FOR THE LIFE AND GROWTH OF FAITH IN A PARISH

This prayer may be used as a symbolic experience for the pastoral council, or as a way to commission an implementation group for a specific task. In preparation, have ready some soil in a sack, a container with water, a flower pot, and some seeds. For larger groups, make appropriate modifications.

Begin with a simple introduction to the purpose of the gathering. Invite people to quiet themselves in the presence of God. Play quiet music for a few minutes until the room is still. (The music may continue throughout the time of prayer.) When the group is ready, the leader begins.

Leader: *Hold the sack of soil up for all to see and pray as follows:*
Blessed are you, Lord our God, Creator of the Universe, who has given us the rich soil of the gospels and the treasures of our faith as Catholics. In the symbol of this ordinary dirt, help us to loosen the soil of our hearts so that our parish may be a fertile garden where faith can grow in all your people.

All: Blessed be God forever.

Leader: *Hold the cup of water up for all to see and pray as follows:*
Blessed are you, Lord our God, Creator of the Universe, who has called us by name in baptism and renewed us in the anointing of the Spirit. In the symbol of this water, help us experience your gift of Living Water in our parish, that all who come to us may find true refreshment and support for life.

All: Blessed be God forever.

Leader: *Pour the water into the soil, and mix them together. Then pray:*
By the blending of these two sources of life, help us understand that the Kingdom of God is a work of both heaven and earth. Let us toil together, neither afraid of getting our hands dirty nor fleeing the inevitable rain. Commit us to the work of your Kingdom, Creator God, now and in the days to come.

All: Amen.

Leader: *Open the seed packet and ask someone to plant the seeds. Then pray:*
Blessed are you, Lord our God, who has planted your life deep within each of us. We commend these fragile seeds, containing new life, to this soil and water. Nurture them and nurture us, as we strive to grow the faith life of our parish. May they and we be strong and bear much fruit.

All: Blessed be God forever.

Leader:	Now let us pray for our parish—the hopes and dreams we have for its life and growth—in petition for what we yet desire—and in gratitude for the blessings we already know. Our response is: "Blessed be God forever."
All:	*Spontaneous prayers for the life of the parish, the people, and the council*

When prayer is naturally finished, join hands and recite the Our Father.

TRANSFORMING THE PARISH CHURCH OF THE WINEMAKER

Invitation to Prayer

Leader: Let us, like God's field, open our hearts to receive the grace of this evening.

All: We open ourselves to the planting and the harvesting of the vineyard of the Lord.

Leader: Glory be to the Father, and to the Son, and to the Holy Spirit,

All: As it was in the beginning, is now and ever shall be, world without end. Amen.

Opening Prayer

Leader: Let us pray:
O God, you are the field and you are the vine, you are the farmer and you are the vintner. Continue to loosen the hard soil of our hearts and to plant your Word in us. Keep us attached to your vine, that our branches might bear much fruit. Transform us into the choice wine of your Kingdom, patient with the fermentation, and filled with joy at the outpouring of your Spirit. We pray this in the name of that Spirit and of Jesus, the Lord, who with you are one God, forever and ever.

All: Amen.

Reading

Reader: A reading from the Gospel of Matthew (Matt 9:17)

People do not put new wine into old wineskins. Otherwise the skins burst, the wine spills out, and the skins are ruined. Rather, they pour new wine into fresh wineskins, and both are preserved.

The Gospel of the Lord.

All: Praise to you, Lord Jesus Christ.

Reflection

Someone may prepare a reflection on the winemaking process or the group may talk informally about what they know. Considerations may include: condi-

tions for growing good fruit, varieties of grapes, "imperfections," degree of ripeness, crushing the grapes, fermentation, sampling and determining the "right time" for bottling, enjoying the fruits of the labor. After some information about winemaking is presented, then share the following reflections:

REVISIONING THE PARISH PASTORAL COUNCIL presents a new model for parish life. As those involved in the preparation of the new wine, what challenges have lured you back to old wineskins or made you hesitant about the fermentation process? What hopes have inspired you to enter the process, regardless of the difficulties you have encountered? As you think about winemaking in your parish, by analogy, what conditions are needed to produce quality fruit? What needs to be done to transform attitudes of mind and heart into new wineskins?

Intercessions

Leader: Each petition concludes with "from old wineskins to new."
The response will be: Transform us by your Spirit.

Reader: From worries about buildings and budgets to hopes for pastoral life, from old wineskins to new,

From private Catholics to a People of God with a mission, from old wineskins to new,

From the "same old" people who do everything to numerous empowered implementers, from old wineskins to new,

From the duty of going to Mass, to full participation in Eucharist at the center of parish life, from old wineskins to new,

From committees and fundraisers to a parish community of stewardship, from old wineskins to new,

From child-focused religious education to total parish growth in faith and life, from old wineskins to new,

From a "let Father do it" attitude to collaborative and competent leadership, from old wineskins to new,

From parochialism and exclusivity to an open evangelizing community of service, from old wineskins to new,

From factions and interest groups to a parish of unity in diversity, from old wineskins to new,

From fear of change to courageous acceptance of Jesus' vision for our parish, from old wineskins to new,

Leader: Let us now join hands and pray for the coming of God's reign, as Jesus taught us: Our Father…

O God, continue to bless the parish and guide our work in preparing new wineskins to receive the new wine, the outpouring of your transforming Spirit. May our parish community be filled with joy and faith and celebrate your Kingdom forever and ever. Amen.

SPRING REFLECTION FOR PASTORAL COUNCILS

Invitation to Prayer

Leader: Christ Jesus is risen from the dead.

All: Alleluia! Alleluia! Alleluia!

Leader: He lives, no more to die.

All: Alleluia! Alleluia! Alleluia!

Leader: Stay with us, Risen Lord.

All: Alleluia! Alleluia! Alleluia!

Opening Hymn

Choose an Easter hymn familiar to the group.

Opening Prayer

Leader: Let us pray:
Risen Lord, in this Easter season we gather in your name to celebrate with joy the promise of eternal life. But sometimes we struggle to believe. Be with us now on our own journeys to Emmaus. Walk with us. Teach us your Word. And reveal your presence to us in community and communion. Be our hidden companion on this lifelong journey, until we rise to Easter glory ourselves, and come to dwell with you, who with the Father and the Spirit are God, forever and ever. Amen.

Reading

Narrator: A reading based on the Gospel of Luke (24:13-35)

Narrator: Now that very day two of the disciples were going to a village seven miles from Jerusalem called Emmaus, and they were talking about all the things that had occurred. And it happened that while they were conversing and debating, Jesus himself drew near and walked with them, but their eyes were prevented from recognizing him.

Jesus: What are you discussing as you walk along?

Disciple 1: Are you the only visitor to Jerusalem who does not know of the things that have taken place there these days?

Jesus: What sort of things?

Disciple 2: The things that happened to Jesus the Nazarene who was a prophet mighty in deed and word before God and all the people.

Disciple 1: How our chief priests and rulers both handed him over to a sentence of death and crucified him.

Disciple 2: We were hoping that he would be the one to redeem Israel; and besides all this, it is now the third day since this took place.

Disciple 1: Some women from our group have astounded us; they were at the tomb early this morning and did not find his body; they came back and reported that they had indeed seen a vision of angels who announced that he was alive.

Disciple 2: Then some of us went to the tomb and found things just as the women had described, but him they did not see.

Jesus: Oh, how foolish you are! How slow of heart to believe all that the prophets spoke! Was it not necessary that the Messiah should suffer these things and enter into his glory?

Narrator: Then beginning with Moses and all the prophets, he interpreted to them what referred to him in all the scriptures. As they approached the village to which they were going, he gave the impression that he was going on farther.

Disciple 1: Stay with us, for it is nearly evening and the day is almost over.

Narrator: So he went in to stay with them. And it happened that, while he was with them at table, he took bread, said the blessing, broke it and gave it to them. With that their eyes were opened and they recognized him but he vanished from sight.

Disciple 2: Were not our hearts burning within us while he spoke to us on the way and opened the scriptures to us?

Disciple 1: Indeed they were. Let us return to Jerusalem with all haste.

Reflection

- On our corporate journey of the past year, what have we been talking about?

- When have we been confused? Discouraged? Excited? Wanting more?
- When have we sat down together in the Lord's name? At the Lord's table?
- When have we found our hearts burning?
- In what moments have we recognized the Lord's presence with us?

Intercessions

Choose a response and mention your prayer petitions spontaneously. Conclude with the Our Father.

Closing Hymn

Sing a final verse or two of the opening hymn.

FOR SEEKING IMPLEMENTATION GROUPS

Invitation to Prayer

Leader: Let us bring ourselves into the presence of our God who is always present to us. Let us lay down the busy-ness of our day, and become aware of the easy yoke and light burden Jesus Christ invites us to bear. Let us enter into this time of prayer and reflection with quiet attentiveness.

Pause for a few moments of silence.

Leader: We begin now in the name of the Father, + and of the Son and of the Holy Spirit. Amen.

Opening Hymn

Select a hymn on discipleship such as:

Go, Make of All Disciples
Lift High the Cross
City of God
As a Fire Is Meant for Burning
Church of God
Glorious in Majesty
Bring Forth the Kingdom

Opening Prayer

Leader: Let us pray:
Lord God, you have called us to be your disciples and to feed your people. We cannot do it alone. Be with us and guide us in uncovering the gifts of our parishioners and inviting them to be part of the mission of Jesus and of our parish. Touch hearts with openness to this invitation given in his name, and help us be sources of energy and encouragement. We pray this in the name of Jesus, who with you and the Holy Spirit are one God, forever and ever. Amen.

Reading

Reader: A reading from the Gospel of John (John 6:1-13)

Now Jesus went across the Sea of Galilee. A large crowd followed him, because they saw the signs he was performing on the sick.

Jesus went up on the mountain, and there he sat down with his disciples. The Jewish feast of Passover was near. When Jesus raised his eyes and saw that a large crowd was coming to him, he said to Philip, "Where can we buy enough food for them to eat?" He said this to test him, because he himself knew what he was going to do.

Philip answered him, "Two hundred days' wages worth of food would not be enough for each of them to have a little bit." One of his disciples, Andrew, the brother of Simon Peter, said to him, "There is a boy here who has five barley loaves and two fish; but what good are these for so many?" Jesus said, "Have the people recline."

Now there was a great deal of grass in that place. So the men reclined, about five thousand in number. Then Jesus took the loaves, gave thanks, and distributed them to those who were reclining, and also as much of the fish as they wanted. When they had had their fill, he said to his disciples, "Gather the fragments left over, so that nothing will be wasted." So they collected them, and filled twelve wicker baskets with fragments from the five barley loaves that had been more than they could eat.

The Gospel of the Lord.

All: Praise to you, Lord Jesus Christ.

Reflections

- What, if anything, did you hear in this reading that you hadn't noticed before?

- Why do you suppose the child did not hesitate to share his food with the people?

- In light of this gospel story, how can we inspire our parishioners to share their gifts and talents with the parish?

Intercessions

Use this opportunity to pray for the needs of the parish and the world. Conclude with the Our Father.

Closing Prayer

Leader: Let us pray:
So often, Lord Jesus, we look around our parish and say, "What good is the little we have among so many?" We fear that your work will not get accomplished because no one will come forward to assist in doing it. Give us new insight into those with the gifts we need for your mission. Give us wisdom and enthusiasm as we invite them to share their time and talents with the rest of the parish. Do not let us become discouraged, but remind us that you always provide for us. With faith, we know that all will be filled and more will remain than we ever had. We pray this in your name, Jesus Christ, who feeds and cares for us forever and ever. Amen.

AT THE TIME OF EVALUATING THE PASTORAL PLAN

Invitation to Prayer

Leader: Jesus Christ is the light of the world.

All: A light which no darkness can extinguish.

Leader: Glory be to the Father, and to the Son, and to the Holy Spirit

All: As it was in the beginning, is now and ever shall be, world without end. Amen.

Opening Hymn

Select a hymn on service, mission or thanksgiving, such as:

You Walk along Our Shoreline
Come, Ye Thankful People, Come
Lord Whose Love in Humble Service
Glorious in Majesty
Those Who Love and Those Who Labor
The Church of Christ in Every Age

Opening Prayer

Leader: Let us pray:
O God, you have invited us to participate in the mission of Jesus Christ in our own time and place. You called us individually and as a people to be your sons and daughters; you called us all to be one. Gather us now, and shelter us in the boat of your Church. Grant us the grace of your presence as we review how we have addressed the mission you entrusted to us. We make this prayer through Christ our Lord. Amen.

Reading

Reader: A reading derived from the gospels of Matthew and Mark (Matt 9:35-38, 10:1; Mark 6:30-32)

Now Jesus went around to all the towns and villages in the vicinity of Galilee, teaching in their synagogues, proclaiming the Good News of the Kingdom, and curing every disease and illness. At the sight of the crowds, his heart was moved with pity for them because they were troubled and abandoned, like sheep without a shepherd. Then he said to his disciples, "The harvest is abundant but the laborers are few; so ask the master of the harvest to send out laborers for his harvest."

Then he summoned his twelve disciples and gave them authority over unclean spirits. He instructed them and sent them out two by two . . .

Upon their return, the apostles gathered together with Jesus and reported all they had done and taught. He said to them, "Come away by yourselves to a deserted place and rest awhile." People were coming and going in great numbers, and they had no opportunity even to eat. So they went off in the boat by themselves to a deserted place.

The Gospel of the Lord.

All: Praise to You, Lord Jesus Christ.

Reflections

Jesus had a deep conviction about his mission and a zeal for accomplishing it. But he knew he could not do it alone. So he recruited and commissioned his followers to extend that mission of teaching the Good News and healing people's ills. On their return from their "commissioned ministry," the disciples were invited by Jesus to come away for a while to talk about what they had accomplished and to rest at the conclusion of their activity.

- What kinds of things do you think the apostles talked about with Jesus and one another when they returned from their ministry?
- Imagine that Jesus has invited you here today to review what you've done in leadership ministry for the past year or so. What would you share with him and your co-disciples?
- Thinking about people in the parish who are hard at work implementing objectives, what would you invite them to talk about with you at this point in the year?
- Why do you think it is important to take time to have this kind of conversation in a life of service to God's people?

At the end of this "evaluation" between Jesus and his disciples, while they were anticipating more quiet time alone with Jesus, their boat pulled in to the shore and they were met by people hungering for the Gospel and for healing. Jesus began immediately to serve them, despite the apostles' desire that they be sent away. Rather, Jesus told them that it was time to pick up the ministry that always needs to be done and to start again.

Intercessions

As we pray for the people in our parish, try to put names and faces on the "crowd." We will be praying in general terms, but our parishioners are unique people and special to God. Think of them and pray for them in particular. *(Individuals may take turns leading the groups of intercessions.)*

Leader: Let us pray in gratitude for all those who implement the mission of Jesus and the mission of our parish by serving others:

1. For ministers of worship:
   for musicians, lectors, eucharistic ministers, ushers and greeters;
   for those who participate in liturgy as members of the assembly;
   for sacristans and planners, for presiders and homilists;
   and for all those who enhance the prayer life of our parishes
   we pray to the Lord.

2. For ministers of the word:
   for RCIA and sacramental preparation teams;
   for catechists who work with all ages and for those who teach in Catholic schools;
   for parents who lovingly pass on the faith to their children;
   for participants in faith sharing and Bible study groups;
   and for all those who love God's word and act on it in daily ways
   we pray to the Lord.

3. For ministers who build community:
   for parish groups and organizations;
   for those who prepare parish bulletins and newsletters;
   for those who plan activities and seek out others;
   for those who remind us about and look out for the "excluded" in our parishes;
   for kitchen crews and festival workers;
   and for all those who bring people together and unite them in the love of Christ
   we pray to the Lord.

4. For ministers of service:
   for those who visit the sick and homebound;
   for those who work with the poor and needy;
   for those who protest injustice or who influence public policy;
   for St. Vincent de Paul societies and the Ladies of Charity;
   for those who speak with prophetic voices;
   and for all those who act with justice and compassion
   we pray to the Lord.

5. For good stewards:
   for finance councils, money counters, and maintenance personnel;
   for assembly participants who share ideas and commitments;
   for faithful contributors to the Sunday collection and to special appeals;
   for all volunteers and supporters of parish activities;
   for stewards of the faith and stewards of service;
   and for all those who gratefully pass on the treasure of the Church to the next generation
   we pray to the Lord.

6. For those called to the ministry of leadership:
   for pastoral councils across the diocese;
   for facilitators, conveners, recorders, transition, and spiritual formation teams;
   for pastors and parish staff members;
   for leaders of implementation groups;
   for leaders of ministry groups, parish organizations, youth and service groups;
   for organizers, motivators, and inviters;
   and for all those who engage and empower others, and lead them to the Kingdom of God
   we pray to the Lord.

7. For evangelizers:
   for those who share stories of faith, extend hospitality, and welcome strangers;
   for those whose lives witness to the presence of Christ in family and workplace;
   for those who plan and participate in renewal efforts;
   for those who reach out to the disillusioned and inactive;
   for those whose enthusiasm for the Gospel creates zeal in others;
   and for all those who proclaim the Good News in word and deed
   we pray to the Lord.

Leader: Let us pray:
Loving Lord of the Harvest, in your son Jesus Christ you have given us an example of tireless service to the People of God. Now bless all those of our parish who follow in his footsteps. Inspire others to hear your call and respond with a commitment to furthering his mission in our time. Build us up into his Body, the Church, united in one faith through one baptism. We pray this in the name of Jesus, who with you and the Holy Spirit are one God, forever and ever.

All: Amen.

PRAYER FOR DISCERNING PASTORAL COUNCIL LEADERS

Invitation to Prayer

Leader: Come, Holy Spirit, fill the hearts of your faithful

All: And kindle in them the fire of your love.

Leader: Send forth your Holy Spirit and they shall be created

All: And you will renew the face of the earth.

Opening Hymn

Choose a familiar hymn to the Holy Spirit.

Opening Prayer

Leader: Let us pray:
Come, O Holy Spirit of the living God, and show us your ways. Guide our discernment of those who are called to the ministry of leadership in our parish. Grant us wisdom to know our gifts. Call us to put those gifts at the service of your people. Give us zeal and holy courage to respond generously to your invitation. And grant your grace to all in our faith community as they seek to live out the mission of Jesus. We pray this in his name, who with you and the sustaining Father are one God, forever and ever. Amen.

Reading

Reader: A reading derived from the letter of Paul to the Romans (Rom 12)

Now I urge you: do not conform yourself to this age, but be transformed by the renewal of your mind, that you may discern what is the will of God, what is good and pleasing and perfect. For by the grace given to me I tell all of you not to think of yourselves more highly than you ought to think, but to think soberly, each according to the measure of faith that God has apportioned. For as in one body we have many parts, and all the parts do not have the same function, so we, though many, are one body in Christ and individually parts of one another.

Since we have gifts that differ according to the grace given to us, let us exercise them: if prophecy, in proportion to the faith; if ministry, in ministering; if one is a teacher, in teaching; if one exhorts, in exhortation; if one contributes, in generosity; if one is a leader, with diligence; if one does acts of mercy, with cheerfulness.

Let love be sincere; hate what is evil, hold on to what is good; love one another with mutual affection; anticipate one another in showing honor. Do not grow slack in zeal, be fervent in spirit, serve the Lord. Rejoice in hope, endure in affliction, persevere in prayer. Contribute to the needs of the holy ones, exercise hospitality. Have the same regard for one another; do not be haughty but associate with the lowly; do not be wise in your own estimation. If possible, on your part, live at peace with all.

The Word of the Lord.

All: Thanks be to God.

Reflection

Consider quietly for a few moments and then share with those gathered:

Of all the advice Paul gives us in this reading, what line or phrase seems most significant to you at this time? Why?

DISCERNMENT PROCESS

Those who are being considered to fill the role of council member are asked to address several questions, without judgment, interrogation, or interruption by others in the room. Respectful listening and continuing prayer to the Spirit mark this time.

Part I:

Each person introduces himself or herself. Candidates' introductions should include the following information:

- Name
- Length of time as a member of the parish
- Ways in which they have been involved in the parish over the years
- The church activity, ministry, or service they found most rewarding

After each person speaks, the group affirms and prays for him or her.

Leader: Let us pray in gratitude for the life of ________________________ and all the gifts s/he has already shared with this faith community. May God continue to lead her/him in discipleship and service to God's people.

All: Amen! The grace of our Lord Jesus Christ, the love of God the Father and the fellowship of the Holy Spirit be with you.

Part II:

Each person answers these questions:

- What gifts do you have for the ministry of leadership?
- What moved you to offer them to the work of the parish pastoral council?

Part III:

Each person chooses one of the following questions and answers it:

- What one thing do you think would make the biggest difference in the spiritual life of our parish?
- What one thing do you think is the greatest need in the parish?
- What is the greatest stumbling block to moving our parish forward?
- If you could give all the people in our parish an injection of some spiritual gift, what would it be and why?
- What part of our mission statement is most challenging to you? Why?

After the candidates have spoken, time is allotted for questions and answers. After this, people may withdraw their names from consideration, although they should be invited to stay with the group through the rest of the process and to participate in the discernment.

Then the group begins the discernment process for new members. Each person identifies several individuals whose gifts would bring a complementary presence to the present council. They then discuss the reasons for their choices.

If it appears that certain persons are clearly selected by the group, their names are listed. Continuing rounds of identifying persons with their gifts in relationship to the council are held until the full number of council members is selected.

If it appears that certain persons are discerned as equally possessing the needed gifts and the group cannot make a choice, after additional prayer, the member may be chosen in a caucus among those whose names are still being considered.

A final affirmation of consensus is voiced and a closing prayer of blessing and gratitude is offered.

Closing Prayer

Leader: Let us pray:
In gratitude for your presence with us, O Holy Spirit, we bring you thanks and praise.

Now bless these, your servants, as they assume the ministry of leadership among our parishioners. Give them unity, vision, wisdom, and a great love for you and your people. We pray this in the name of Jesus, our model and our shepherd, now and forever. Amen.

Reader: A reading based on the second letter of Paul to the Corinthians (2 Cor 9:1, 11-15)

Now about your service to God's holy ones; I know your eagerness. You are being enriched in every way for your generosity, which through us produces thanksgiving to God, for the administration of this public service is not only supplying the needs of the holy ones, but is also overflowing in many acts of gratitude. Through the evidence of this service, you are glorifying God in your fidelity to the Gospel of Jesus Christ and the generosity of your contribution to God's people and to all others. In prayer for your good, they hope in you because of the surpassing grace of God. Thanks be to God for such an indescribable gift!

The Word of the Lord.

All: Thanks be to God.

Intercessions

Leader: Now let us pray for our parish and all the future holds for us. The response will be: Hear our prayer, O Holy Spirit of God.

Reader: For leaders of the Church throughout the world, for our Holy Father Pope _______________, for our Bishop _______________, for Fr. _______________, our pastor, and for members of this pastoral council, that the Spirit of wisdom and discipleship may guide their service of God's people, we pray to the Lord:

All: *Pray aloud with spontaneous petitions for the intentions of the group.*

Reader: For all those who have gone before us in this community of faith, that their good example and fruitful work may be blessed with an eternity of joy in the heavenly kingdom, we pray to the Lord:

Leader: We pray now in the words that Jesus gave us: Our Father. . .

May almighty God bless us, the Father + and the Son and the Holy Spirit.

All: Amen.

Leader: Go in peace, to love and serve the Lord in one another.

All: Thanks be to God.

Leader: Let us conclude by exchanging the greeting of peace.

Those selected to be on the council complete the signing of the "Willingness to Serve" form (see page 197). Their names are announced to the parish as soon as possible.

Reflecting on the Essential Elements of Parish Life in Prayer

During times of council prayer, or in leading prayer with parish groups responsible for carrying out goals related to different elements, the following quotes may provide helpful material for sharing. Can you think of a question or two which would lead your group into fruitful reflection on these quotations?

Evangelization

"Evangelization is in fact the grace and vocation proper to the Church, her deepest identity. She exists in order to evangelize, that is to say, in order to preach and teach, to be the channel of the gift of grace, to reconcile sinners with God and to perpetuate Christ's sacrifice in the Mass, which is the memorial of his death and glorious Resurrection."

Evangelii Nuntiandi (On Evangelization in the Modern World), 14.
Pope Paul VI. 1975.

REFLECTION QUESTION:

Worship

"In most parishes, Sunday is most likely the only time that many Catholics come into formal contact with the Church as Church. For this reason, the Sunday Eucharist needs to be a high priority in the life of the community. This demands a commitment of time, energy, and resources to assure that the Sunday Eucharist is and remains the focal point of the community. For it is here that the community comes to celebrate its life of faith; it is here where the Church is renewed to continue its mission."

Sunday Eucharist: Source and Summit of Parish Life. Guidelines for Evaluating the Quality and Number of Sunday Masses. Diocese of Greensburg. 1995.

REFLECTION QUESTION:

Word

"Catechesis [encompasses] the totality of the Church's efforts to make disciples, to help men believe that Jesus is the Son of God so that believing they might have life in his name, and to educate and instruct them in this life, thus building up the body of Christ (cf. John Paul II, apostolic exhortation, *Catechesi tradendae* [*CT*] 1; 2). . . . Catechesis is built on . . . the initial proclamation of the Gospel . . . to arouse faith; examination of the reasons for belief; experience of Christian living; celebration of the sacraments; integration into the ecclesial community; and apostolic and missionary witness (*CT* 18)."

Catechism of the Catholic Church, 4, 6. USCC. 1994.

REFLECTION QUESTION:

Service

"The central message is simple: our faith is profoundly social. We cannot be truly 'Catholic' unless we hear and heed the church's call to serve those in need and work for justice and peace. . . . We see the parish dimension of social ministry not as an added burden, but as part of what keeps a parish alive and makes it truly Catholic. Effective social ministry helps the parish not only do more, but be more—more of a reflection of the Gospel, more of a worshipping and evangelizing people, more of a faithful community. It is an essential part of parish life."

Communities of Salt and Light: Reflections on the Social Ministry of the Parish, 3, 1. U.S. Bishops' Statement. 1993.

REFLECTION QUESTION:

Community

"By virtue of this catholicity, each part contributes its own gifts to other parts and to the entire Church, so that the whole and each of the parts are strengthened by the common sharing of all things and by the common effort to achieve fullness in unity. . . . Finally, between all the various parts of the Church, there is a bond of intimate communion whereby spiritual riches, apostolic workers and temporal resources are shared. . . . All are called to this catholic unity of the people of God which prefigures and promotes universal peace."

Lumen Gentium (Dogmatic Constitution on the Church), Chapter II, 13.

REFLECTION QUESTION:

Stewardship

"What identifies a steward? Safeguarding material and human resources and using them responsibly is one answer; so is generous giving of time, talent, and treasure. But being a Christian steward means more. As Christian stewards, we receive God's gifts gratefully, cultivate them responsibly, share them lovingly in justice with others, and return them with increase to the Lord."

To Be a Christian Steward: A Summary of the U.S. Bishops' Pastoral Letter on Stewardship, 45. USCC. 1992.

REFLECTION QUESTION:

Leadership

"Pastoral council members ought to be individuals of faith who are capable of leading the parish in the discernment, expression, and fulfillment of its mission. Ideally, they are people of vision, open to the workings of the Holy Spirit in and through themselves, while having a deep respect and openness for the workings of the Spirit in others."

Revisioning the Parish Pastoral Council, 160.

REFLECTION QUESTION:

Suggestions for Shaping Reflection Questions

Here are some useful suggestions for both scripture sharing and sharing on other documents.

When posing a reflection question, it is sometimes helpful to do it in several stages. The first stage simply asks what the text is saying. It seeks a factual response and gives group members the opportunity to reconstruct the passage in their own words. "What did you hear in the text?"

The second stage usually asks for interpretation, meaning, or application. It is more personal and requires the people to bring their faith and experience into dialog with the text. "What does this mean to you? When have you experienced something like this?"

Finally, the reflection can extend to the parish situation. "To what is this text calling the council in its service of the parish?"

As councils become more familiar with faith sharing, they may be able to move quickly to the personal/reflective and the application levels.

Avoid asking questions which can be answered with a simple yes or no. Encourage members to speak not in general terms—about "them" or "someone"—but to speak using "I" statements, articulating what they believe, think, feel, or understand personally.

Spending time preparing the reflection questions will help in shaping purposeful discussions and guide the participants to worthwhile conversation. Nothing is as deadening as hearing the leader beg, "Does anyone have anything to say?" A good question opens up not only the text, but the people who are in relationship with both the text and one another.

CONSENSUS

WHY CONSENSUS?

REVISIONING THE PARISH PASTORAL COUNCIL is rooted and has its goal the mission of Christ: "Go therefore and make disciples of all nations" (Matt 28:19). Pastoral councils that are committed to this mission never lose sight of their need to seek God's will.

Councils are always in the search for wisdom, for the course of action that has the best hope of being what God wants for the parish. When members of the pastoral council come together to make decisions, they are aware that as a parish leadership body they have the responsibility to weigh and judge in the light of God's will. They must ask themselves these challenging questions:

How can we, the people of God, know with the certitude of faith that we are making the right decision?

How can we discover not our own will for God but God's will for us?

The consensus model of decision making is appropriate when we truly believe that God has an investment in our parish. After valid information has been obtained, we surround it with prayer and allow the truth to be known in and through the leadership body, including the pastor. Parish members have a great deal to offer to the parish—but they need leaders who have first taken the risk to trust the wisdom of God within the Body of Christ.

The Consensus Process

What is consensus?

Consensus is group process for decision making in which all come to a common understanding and agree to support the decision of the whole.

What are the "non-negotiables" of consensus?

Consensus
- is built on prayer
- seeks the will of God, not "my" will
- is based on mutual trust among persons making the decision
- honors the teachings of the scriptures and the Church

What is not involved in consensus?

Consensus does not involve
- majority rule (no votes are taken)
- compromise (people don't give in to keep the peace)
- competition (there are no winners and losers)
- quick decisions (working through to consensus takes time)
- dependence on the leader (all engage in the discussion and come to a decision)

What are the four steps of a the consensus process?

1. ***Input***
   - Issue is clearly stated.
   - Background information is presented.
   - Opportunity for clarification is given.
2. ***Discussion***
   - Facilitator introduces issue, others respond. Facilitator keeps discussion on the issue.
   - When most viewpoints have been expressed, facilitator tests for consensus.
3. ***Reflection***
   - Does what is proposed support the Gospel?
   - In light of the parish mission statement, will this be good for the entire parish?
   - Can each of us live with this and support this?
4. ***Review***
   - Summarize the issue, basic background, areas of agreement and disagreement, statement of consensus reached.
   - If there is no consensus, continue to discuss the problematic areas.

What can be done when consensus is difficult to reach?

- If the discussion is "going around in circles," drop the matter and continue the meeting. Return to the issue later.
- If there seems to be missing information, do further research and gather more data before trying to complete the consensus process. Postpone further discussion until all have had the opportunity for prayer and reflection time.

What if I'm the one who's outside the circle of agreement?

- Are you considering what is best for all?
- Do you understand all the data presented?
- Have you carefully justified your reasons for disagreeing?
- Can you say, "Well, I don't agree completely, but I see the validity of your position and I can live with that"?

What kind of attitudes are harmful and helpful to the process?

HARMFUL	HELPFUL
rigidity of opinions	openness
hostile or suspicious attitude	honesty
determination to win	respect for the truth in everyone
sabotaging the process	patience
"Why do we have to do it this way?"	enthusiastic support for outcome—often a brand new idea

When should our council use a formal consensus process?

- Only when discerning major decisions that are intended to establish goals and objectives for the future.
- Not with regard to operational issues or day-to-day decisions. Most of these issues are not brought to the council anyway.

SHAPING CONSENSUS

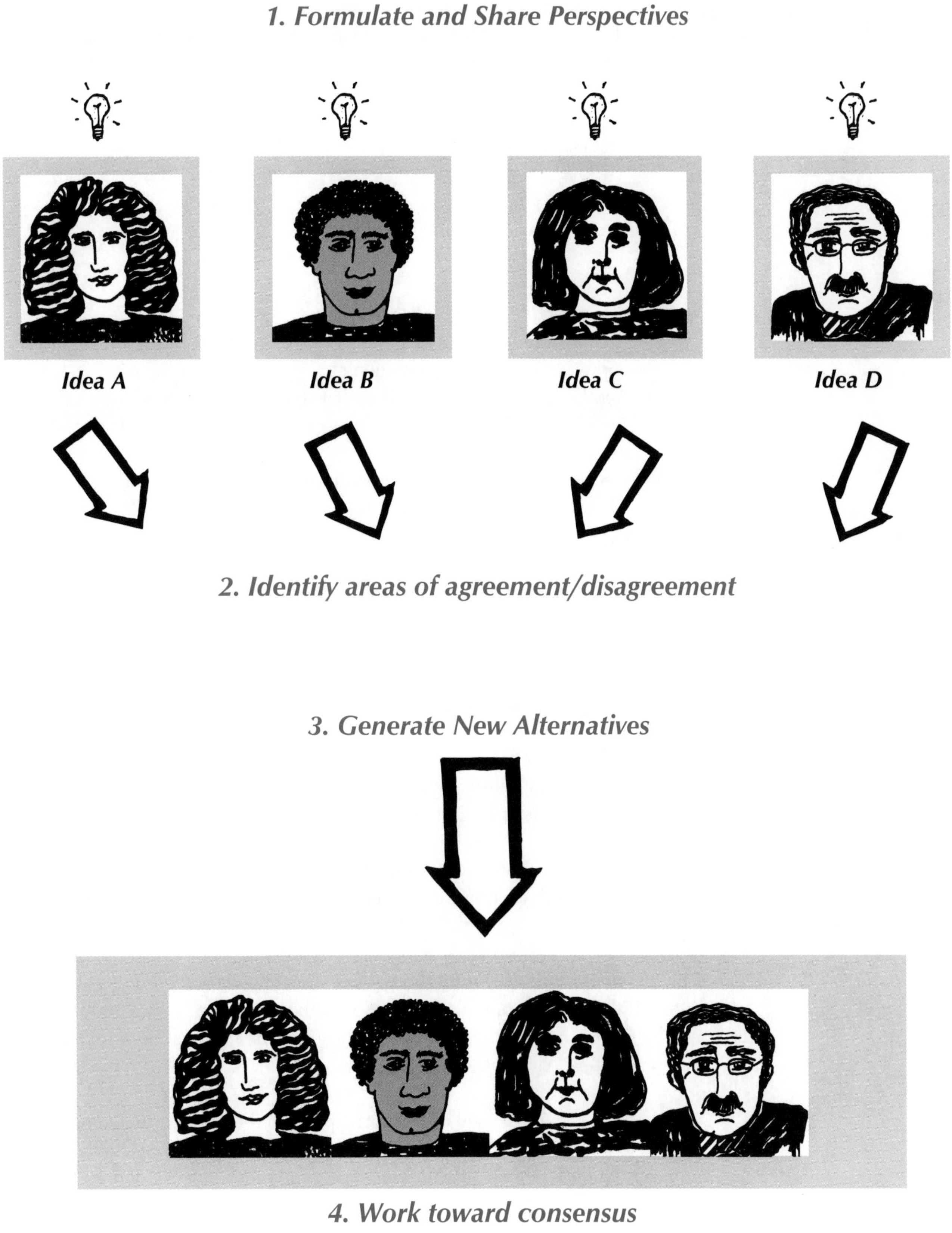

Six Steps for Arriving at Consensus

There are no neat ways for coming to consensus, but here are six steps that can help guide the process. After the issue has been presented and necessary background information has been given, the facilitator:

1. Invites clarifying questions.

2. Summarizes for the council what the issues are.

3. Invites someone to begin discussion.
   - An individual introduces an idea/opinion as to how the issue might be approached (using "I" statements).
   - Another individual responds to that statement (as a good listener would) and adds ideas or reactions of his/her own (using "I" statements).
   - A third individual develops ideas further (using "I" statements), until all have shared their views.

4. Keeps discussion on the topic and, if needed, rephrases complicated or confusing comments.

5. Summarizes points of agreement and points of difference.

6. Noting that consensus is possible, "tests" for consensus by asking if there is anything else of importance to be offered that has not been said. Or, noting that there are serious areas of disagreement, invites individuals to be ready to state their position on the issue, give reasons for their position, and perhaps present alternate solutions.

The discussion continues until the areas of disagreement are reduced or eliminated. If the council cannot reach consensus because more information is needed, a person or group is delegated to gather the information within a certain time frame, e.g., by the next meeting.

Consensus is achieved when all the participants in the process, including the pastor, agree that they have been heard, are valued for their convictions and are, consequently, able to affirm and support the prevailing position.

A Short Exercise in Coming to Consensus

If your council is just beginning its work together, here is a short exercise that will demonstrate the give and take of a consensus decision. For this "practice" it is more important that you observe the process than that you actually make a final plan.

The following are some possible long-range goals for parish life. Prioritize them according to your present situation and suggest one more objective for each item.

GOAL A: To enrich our worship life with increased participation and expanded prayer opportunities in the parish.

- To upgrade the worship aids in the pews.
-

GOAL B: To make hospitality a visible quality of our parish.

- To establish a "Welcome Booth" at weekend liturgies where newcomers or interested persons can register and/or receive information about the parish.
-

GOAL C: To focus on family life as the primary place for religious formation.

- To establish a yearly intergenerational family retreat.
-

GOAL D: To join with other parishes and churches in our area to rebuild a sense of community through works of justice and peace.

- To sponsor a workshop on organizing for justice and invite area church leaders.
-

II: THE SEVEN ESSENTIAL ELEMENTS OF PARISH LIFE

The Essence of Parish Life

Seven elements form the essence of parish life:

EVANGELIZATION

WORSHIP

WORD

COMMUNITY

SERVICE

STEWARDSHIP

LEADERSHIP

These elements constantly interrelate in parish life, each nurturing and supporting the other. The illustration on the left shows this interrelationship, with the communal celebration of Sunday Eucharist at the center.

Knowing what the seven essential elements are and understanding their interrelationship is central to the functioning of the pastoral council. These elements are what make pastoral councils "pastoral." They keep councils on track as to what they should be praying, planning, and deciding about. When the Code of Canon Law limited the scope of pastoral councils, it freed councils from being responsible for every issue in a parish, from organizing bazaars to authorizing contracts for repair work, from maintaining organizations and calendars to running fundraisers. Now, the agenda of the council is primarily to research, consider, and propose for action those matters considered to be truly "pastoral," those matters that directly relate to the seven elements. For this reason, all council members with the aid of the pastor and professional staff persons need to become informed as to the "theology" of the seven elements.

The Foundations for the Seven Elements of Parish Life

The foundations for the seven elements are discovered by reviewing the Code of Canon Law (canons 528–530) and what is prescribed in terms of normative pastoral activity in every parish. Every pastor is responsible for seeing that the activities listed below are carried out in his parish. Through its collaboration with the pastor, the council, too, shares responsibility for these activities.

1. Announcing the word of God in its entirety to those living in the parish.
2. Instructing lay Christian faithful in the truths of the faith through the homily and through catechetical formation.
3. Fostering works by which the spirit of the Gospel, including issues involving social justice, is promoted.
4. Taking special care for the Catholic education of children and of young adults.
5. Bringing the gospel message to those who have ceased practicing their religion.
6. Seeing to it that the Most Holy Eucharist is the center of the parish assembly of the faithful.
7. Nourishing the Christian faithful through a devout celebration of the sacraments.
8. Bringing the Christian faithful to the practice of family prayer.
9. Bringing the Christian faithful to knowing and active participation in the sacred liturgy.
10. Striving to know the people of the parish by visiting them and sharing their cares, worries, and especially their griefs.
11. Helping the sick, especially those close to death.
12. Making a special effort to seek out the poor, the afflicted, the lonely, those exiled from their own land, and those weighed down with special difficulties.
13. Fostering growth between spouses.
14. Supporting Christian life within the family.
15. Promoting the unity and communion which exists between the parish and both the diocese and the universal Church.

Recognizing and Assessing the Seven Elements in a Parish

What follows are exercises designed to help a parish assess its strengths and discover areas of challenge for each of the seven elements of parish life. This "assessment tool" can be used in a variety of ways:

- Pastoral council members could individually work through the exercises and then share their perspectives with the whole group to get a "feel" for the pastoral state of the parish.
- Pastoral council members could also use the exercises with various groups in the parish, emphasizing particular elements with groups that have them as their foundation (e.g., Liturgy Committee—WORSHIP; Catechetical Leaders—WORD; Parish Organizations—COMMUNITY; St. Vincent de Paul Society—SERVICE; Parish Pastoral Council—LEADERSHIP; Parish Finance Council—STEWARDSHIP).
- Older school-aged children in religious formation classes can use these exercises to learn about the seven elements

Each exercise addresses one of the seven elements and contains:

1. an overview, including the definition of and foundational background for the element,
2. a checklist of "descriptors," characteristics of a parish that is faithfully attending to the development of that element,
3. an evidence section that provides space for listing concrete ways in which one's parish is currently implementing specific items on the checklist, and
4. a challenge section for listing areas that need attention.

The descriptors in each exercise are actually indicators pointing toward concrete ways in which an essential element gets lived out in the parish. Honest discussion about how the element is or is not embodied in the parish is critical. This kind of open, year-to-year dialogue provides the opportunity for councils to look at hard evidence for each element and to address the pastoral areas that need attention in and through the pastoral planning process.

EVANGELIZATION

The term "evangelization" encompasses any way in which a parish continues to spread the Good News of Jesus, especially (though not exclusively) through personal and communal sharing of faith. This proclamation of the message of Christ is the fundamental mission of the Church and every parish. How each parish carries out its mission of evangelization is unique and particular to that community of faith.

Evangelization is predominant in the diagram below because every aspect of parish life contributes to the unfolding of the Kingdom of God through witnessing to gospel values. The local faith community is to be an evangelizing parish, where everything that is done, whether it be "Worship," "Service," "Word," or any other essential element, has as its end the manifestation of the love of God in Christ Jesus.

Pope Paul VI issued the encyclical On Evangelization in the Modern World (*Evangelii Nuntiandi*) in December 1975, a year after the close of the Synod of Bishops on Evangelization. In that document, the Pope reiterated that Evangelization is at the heart of the mission of the Church:

> The Church is born of the evangelizing activity of Jesus and the Twelve. She is the normal, desired, most immediate and most visible fruit of this activity. . .[11]
>
> Evangelization is in fact the grace and vocation proper to the Church, her deepest identity. She exists in order to evangelize, that is to say, in order to preach and teach, to be the channel of the gift of grace, to reconcile sinners with God, and to perpetuate Christ's sacrifice in the Mass, which is the memorial of his death and glorious Resurrection.[12]

In November 1992, the National Conference of Catholic Bishops issued *Go and Make Disciples,* a document that offered a broad context in which parishes could reflect upon their primary mission of evangelization. The bishops offered three general goals for a "national plan and strategy for Catholic evangelization in the United States," goals that are applicable to any pastoral mission:

GOAL I: To bring about in all Catholics such an enthusiasm for their faith that, in living their faith in Jesus, they freely share it with others.

GOAL II: To invite all people in the United States, whatever their social or cultural background, to hear the message of salvation in Jesus Christ so they may come to join us in the fullness of the Catholic faith.

GOAL III: To foster gospel values in our society, promoting the dignity of the human person, the importance of the family, and the common good of our society, so that our nation may continue to be transformed by the saving power of Jesus Christ.[13]

This is the mission of all members of the Church: to practice their faith with enthusiasm, to invite others to share their faith, and to transform society. Evangelization is at the heart of our individual and communal call to bear witness to Christ.

Twenty years after the encyclical's call to evangelization in this modern era, and nearly two thousand years after Christ's mandate to "Go and make disciples of all nations" (Matt 28:19), the Church today reaffirms the fact that evangelization is fundamental to any parish response to the call of God. It is the essential element of the pastoral mission.

EVANGELIZATION IN PARISH LIFE

Descriptors

- ☐ 1. Adults and children are given opportunities for evangelization formation.
- ☐ 2. Newcomers are welcomed into the parish.
- ☐ 3. Efforts are made to reach out to the alienated, the inactive, and the unchurched.
- ☐ 4. Opportunities are provided for small groups to gather and share faith as it relates to their everyday life.
- ☐ 5. The parish has a plan for regular personal visits with parishioners.
- ☐ 6. Parish renewals, evenings of prayer and/or retreat days are planned to enliven and deepen the faith of the people.
- ☐ 7. The public image of the parish is one of hospitality, invitation, and compassion, where no one is excluded.
- ☐ 8. The parish takes steps to influence the values and decisions of the larger community through prophetic action and works of justice and outreach.
- ☐ 9. There is a sense of Christian joy about the Good News of Jesus Christ; it is evident in homilies, in worship, in parish activities, and in outreach efforts.

ASSESSING EVANGELIZATION IN OUR PARISH

Evidence

(A list of the ways in which our parish currently implements specific items on the checklist)

Example: We sponsor a Lenten renewal program every three years.

Challenges

(A list of areas that need attention)

Example: We have no outreach to inactive Catholics, even though 68 percent of our registered parishioners no longer attend Mass regularly.

WORSHIP

The spiritual life of a parish animates its mission. Personal and communal prayer are essential to the building up of the Body of Christ. The worship of the community, in turn, gives expression to its prayerfulness. In the celebration of Sunday Eucharist and in other sacramental and liturgical rites, individuals gather together to manifest a communal proclamation of faith. In doing so, they carry out the mission of evangelization by witnessing the Good News of Jesus Christ to one another and to all.

In the Constitution on the Sacred Liturgy, we read:

> For it is the liturgy through which, especially in the divine sacrifice of the Eucharist, the work of our redemption is accomplished, and it is through the liturgy, especially, that the faithful are enabled to express in their lives and manifest to others the mystery of Christ and the real nature of the true Church.[14]

Worship itself *is* evangelization, a communal witness to the sovereignty of God, the abiding presence of Jesus Christ, and the power of the Holy Spirit at work in the Church. Worship gives expression to the faith of the community and its degree of commitment to furthering the Kingdom of God.

In the Decree on the Apostolate of the Laity, we read:

> Nourished by their active participation in the liturgical life of their community, they [the laity] engage zealously in its apostolic works; they draw [others] towards the Church who had been perhaps very far away from it; they ardently cooperate in the spread of the Word of God, particularly by catechetical instruction; by their expert assistance they increase the efficacy of the care of souls as well as of the administration of the goods of the Church.[15]

Thus we see how the worship of the community interfaces with and supports all the other essential elements of the pastoral mission.

WORSHIP IN PARISH LIFE

Descriptors

- ☐ 1. The Sunday Eucharist is a priority in the life of the parish and is celebrated with full and active participation of the parishioners.
- ☐ 2. Competent individuals are responsible for every aspect of liturgical celebrations.
- ☐ 3. Parishioners serve in many liturgical roles at liturgy.
- ☐ 4. Liturgical ministers are well trained and effective in their ministries.
- ☐ 5. Preaching is directly related to the scriptures and to the real life experience of the people.
- ☐ 6. The worship space is able to accommodate the rites of the Church in a dignified and liturgically suitable manner.
- ☐ 7. Liturgical art and environment are marked by noble simplicity.
- ☐ 8. Worship aids are contemporary and in good condition.
- ☐ 9. Quality in music, including instruments, musicians, and hymn selection, enables the assembly to participate in sung prayer.
- ☐ 10. All the sacraments are celebrated regularly, with attention given to making them true expressions of the life of the parish.
- ☐ 11. Liturgy of the Word with Children is celebrated with young members of the parish.
- ☐ 12. Devotional prayer is encouraged, but does not interfere with the primary sacramental celebrations of the parish.

ASSESSING WORSHIP IN OUR PARISH

Evidence

(A list of the ways in which our parish currently implements specific items on the checklist)

Example: We have seventeen parishioners who are lectors and thirteen of them attended a diocesan workshop last fall.

Challenges

(A list of areas that need attention)

Example: Some of our substitute organists are not strong musicians and the hymns drag so the people don't sing.

WORD

Spiritual formation is the ongoing process of maturation and growth on the Christian journey. As individuals and as a community of faith, Christians are called to an ever-deepening relationship with Christ. Growing in that love relationship, gaining insight into the nature of God, the incarnate Word of Christ the Son, the power and action of the Holy Spirit, and the continual revelation of God's Word in the Church constitute this formative process.

The deepening of faith results from echoing God's word, which takes place in a variety of ways and in multiple contexts within the life of the Church. Historically, the word "catechesis" has been used to denote the process of handing on the faith:

> Quite early on, the name *catechesis* was given to the totality of the Church's efforts to make disciples, to help men believe that Jesus is the Son of God so that believing they might have life in his name, and to educate and instruct them in this life, thus building up the body of Christ (cf. John Paul II, apostolic exhortation, *Catechesi tradendae* [*CT*] 1; 2). . . . Catechesis is built on a certain number of elements of the Church's pastoral mission which have a catechetical aspect. . . . They are: the initial proclamation of the Gospel or missionary preaching to arouse faith; examination of the reasons for belief; experience of Christian living; celebration of the sacraments; integration into the ecclesial community; and apostolic and missionary witness (*CT* 18).[16]

Here we see how the element of "Word" interrelates with all the other essential elements of the pastoral mission. By preaching and teaching the word we build communities of faith whose worship, service, stewardship, and leadership all contribute to the underlying element of evangelization.

The spreading of the word takes place in many formal and informal ways within the parish: adult, youth, and children's education and spiritual formation; the Rite of Christian Initiation of Adults (RCIA); sacramental preparation for the sacraments of initiation and marriage; family formation; renewal efforts; and Sunday homilies. These and other means of passing on the message of Jesus Christ are all aspects of "Word" within the community of faith.

THE WORD IN PARISH LIFE

Descriptors

- ☐ 1. The parish catechetical leader has appropriate education, ability, and experience to provide catechist formation and effective administration of religious education efforts.
- ☐ 2. Skilled and knowledgeable persons staff all aspects of parish formation efforts: catechesis, RCIA, sacramental preparation. They are witnesses to the Gospel, active in parish life, and faithful to the teachings of the Church.
- ☐ 3. Adequate funds, resources, staff, and space are allocated to carry out the catechetical efforts of the parish, including Catholic schools.
- ☐ 4. Religious formation or catechesis is planned and evaluated for all in the parish: adults, youth, and children.
- ☐ 5. Strengthening marriages and nurturing the life of families are priorities for the parish.
- ☐ 6. Assistance is provided to help parents understand their roles as ministers to their children in the formation of Christian values.
- ☐ 7. Catechetical efforts present the essential message of Catholic Christianity using models and methodologies which speak to the total development of the believer and lead to faith commitment in action.
- ☐ 8. Sacramental preparation for baptism, confirmation/Eucharist/reconciliation and marriage is parish-based and intergenerational whenever possible.
- ☐ 9. Catholic schools attended by parish children and youth not only provide strong educational programs but also foster Christian community and witness.

ASSESSING THE WORD IN OUR PARISH

Evidence

(A list of the ways in which our parish currently implements specific items on the checklist)

Example: We include parents in all sessions that prepare children for the sacraments.

Challenges

(A list of areas that need attention)

Example: Our catechetical leader has no formal training for the position and cannot help our catechists very much.

COMMUNITY

Community is an essential element of parish life which draws parishioners together in mutual support, activity, celebration, and growth. It is the unity that results when members become involved with one another in all other elements of the pastoral mission. Hence the universal Church is seen to be "a people brought into unity of the Father, the Son and the Holy Spirit."[17]

By joining together in word and worship, evangelization efforts, service to others, stewardship of God's gifts, and shared leadership, members of the parish form a community where life is shared and nurtured. This development is an ongoing process, ever evolving, changing, and responding in new ways to the promptings of the Spirit.

Community is both the basis for and the outgrowth of the pastoral mission. Without a deep and abiding sense of the unity which binds them together in faith, parishioners cannot begin to discern the ways in which God is calling them, collectively, to experience the Kingdom more fully. Likewise, as the parish labors together toward the fulfillment of its mission, bonds of community are continually strengthened and renewed. An experience of Christian community is both a premise and a product of parish life.

A parish is a place where everyone belongs. Inclusivity and mutuality are hallmarks of community. Special efforts to include those who are physically and mentally challenged or those who are otherwise neglected serve to connect a parish to the broader human community. Inclusivity reflects the communal character of the local church (the diocese), the universal Church, and all of humanity under the one God and Creator.

> The one People of God is accordingly present in all the nations of the earth. . . . All the faithful scattered throughout the world are in communion with each other in the Holy Spirit . . ."[18]

From Jesus' invitation to the disciples, to the earliest Christian communities, on down through the millennia to today's parishes, community has been an essential part of Christian life.

Each part contributes its own gifts to other parts and to the whole Church, so that the whole and each of the parts are strengthened by the common sharing of all things and by the common effort to attain to fullness in unity.[19]

Community is the human dynamic through which the mission of the Church is embodied and embraced.

COMMUNITY IN PARISH LIFE

Descriptors

- ☐ 1. The parish recognizes itself as a Christian community, rather than as a purely social or civic organization.
- ☐ 2. Communication among parish leaders and with parishioners is adequate and consistent.
- ☐ 3. There is a good spirit of working together among parish groups and organizations.
- ☐ 4. All parish organizations and activities are broadly inclusive.
- ☐ 5. Organizational activities are in harmony with the parish pastoral plan and respond to the needs of the members, the parish as a whole, the larger community, and the diocese.
- ☐ 6. Programming for parish organizations consistently offers prayer, information, education, entertainment, and hospitality.
- ☐ 7. There is an annual review of the purpose, effectiveness, and need for each parish organization.
- ☐ 8. An effort is made to provide for the special needs of those who might feel excluded from parish life at some point: young people, single adults, minorities, the separated and divorced, single parents, the widowed, the physically or mentally challenged, the homebound, the elderly.
- ☐ 9. The prayer and activity of the parish are outwardly directed, never totally focused on its own life.
- ☐ 10. The parish collaborates with neighboring parishes as appropriate to enhance the mission of the Church.
- ☐ 11. The parish promotes ecumenical relationships and activities.

ASSESSING COMMUNITY IN OUR PARISH

Evidence

(A list of the ways in which our parish currently implements specific items on the checklist)

Example: We have instituted the Weekly Visitors who take communion to the homebound, and share parish news after every weekend Mass.

Challenges

(A list of areas that need attention)

Example: Our parish facilities are not equipped with restrooms accessible to the disabled.

SERVICE

The mission to which Christ calls the Church clearly includes works of charity and justice. Throughout his public ministry, Jesus demonstrated the degree to which we are to be of service to others in need while working to change the social conditions that create such needs. The Church is called both to serve the needs of others and to eradicate the causes of injustice.

Jesus' own mission was characterized from the beginning by what the Church has come to call social ministry—outreach and service to others:

> He came to Nazareth, where he had grown up, and went according to his custom into the synagogue on the sabbath day. He stood up to read and was handed a scroll of the prophet Isaiah. He unrolled the scroll and found the passage where it was written:
> The Spirit of the Lord is upon me,
> because he has anointed me to bring glad tidings to the poor.
> He has sent me to proclaim liberty to captives and recovery of sight
> to the blind, to let the oppressed go free,
> and to proclaim a year acceptable to the Lord. (Luke 4:16-22)

Jesus continually modeled and mandated such service to others as a primary requirement for discipleship.[20] Later, the letter of James (Jas 2:14-17) reminds the early Christian community that faith without service is lifeless. Already the faithful were in need of encouragement to persist in lives of service to others as an important part of their Christian call.

In our own time, the U.S. bishops have issued a clear reminder to the Church of this essential element of service. In their 1993 statement, *Communities of Salt and Light: Reflections on the Social Ministry of the Parish,* they said:

> The central message is simple: our faith is profoundly social. We cannot be truly "Catholic" unless we hear and heed the Church's call to serve those in need and work for justice and peace.
>
> We see the parish dimension of social ministry not as an added burden, but as part of what keeps a parish alive and makes it truly Catholic. Effective social ministry helps the parish not only do more, but be more—more of a reflection of the Gospel, more of a worshiping and evangelizing people, more of a faithful community. It is an essential part of parish life.[21]

With respect to pastoral councils, the document says specifically:

> Councils, in their important planning and advisory functions, can help place social ministry in the center of parish life. Councils can be a means of collaboration and integration, bringing together liturgy, formation, outreach, and action into a sense of common mission. [22]

There can be no fidelity to Christ, his teaching, or his Church without the element of service to others. Clergy and pastoral councils are responsible for calling forth this essential element of the pastoral mission from the faith community.

SERVICE IN PARISH LIFE

Descriptors

☐ 1. The parish focuses on the needs of the human community, beginning with its own members and extending to the poor and marginalized in the local area, the nation, and the world.

☐ 2. The parish makes every effort to accommodate persons with special needs.

☐ 3. Organizations within the parish systematically address particular human needs by sponsoring projects such as food pantries, shelters for the homeless and job assistance for the unemployed, or by supporting other parishes or agencies which have these services.

☐ 4. Programs that minister to the sick, the bereaved, and the homebound are ongoing.

☐ 5. The parish participates in local, national, and international helping efforts.

☐ 6. An organized program of instruction dealing with current issues in the light of Catholic social teaching has been implemented.

☐ 7. Formation efforts at all levels integrate Catholic social teaching.

☐ 8. Participation in political action, voting in local and national elections, involvement in policy-making at local, state, and national levels is encouraged.

☐ 9. Racial and ethnic harmony, peacemaking and non-violence, respect for life at all stages, and the practice of the spiritual and corporal works of mercy are priority areas for study and action in the parish.

☐ 10. Opportunities for collaborative ecumenical activity in the local area are sought out.

☐ 11. The parish coordinator of social ministry has adequate education and experience for the position.

ASSESSING SERVICE IN OUR PARISH

Evidence

(A list of the ways in which our parish currently implements specific items on the checklist)

Example: We work with the Lutherans and Methodists to operate a food pantry.

Challenges

(A list of areas that need attention)

Example: Our parish religious formation program does not include social justice teachings nor provide opportunities for our young people to be involved in witness and service activities.

STEWARDSHIP

Stewardship can be defined simply as making the most responsible use of one's gifts and resources. It necessitates the recognition of life as a gift, bestowed upon each person by God and responded to in a spirit of humility and gratitude.

As Christians initiated into the Church through the sacraments of baptism, confirmation and Eucharist, we become the caretakers of all that God has given to us. As stewards of creation, we are entrusted with the responsibility of caring for God's Kingdom.

Stewardship, for believers, involves the sharing of individual time, talent, and treasure, as well as the commitment of communal resources (temporal, financial, human, etc.) in service to the community of faith. Members will realize their obligation to contribute to the fulfillment of the parish's mission, and will do so willingly and generously by sharing their personal resources.

In their 1992 pastoral letter, *Stewardship: A Disciple's Response,* the U.S. bishops make the following significant points related to stewardship:

> Essentially, stewardship means helping the Church's mission with time, money, and personal resources of all kinds. This sharing is not an option for Catholics who understand what membership in the Church involves. It is a serious duty.
>
> God wishes human beings to be his collaborators in the work of creation, redemption and sanctification; and such collaboration involves stewardship in its most profound sense. Stewardship in an ecclesial setting means cherishing and fostering the gifts of all, while using one's own gifts to serve the community of faith.[23]

A parish that is living out the essential element of stewardship will place a high priority on regular sacrificial giving by its members in the Sunday offertory. The more emphasis a parish places on regular contributions to fund its mission and budget, the less it needs to rely on extraordinary fundraisers such as tickets, bingo, raffles, and other games of chance. While these means are still utilized in some parishes, they do not clearly reflect the biblical understanding of stewardship, which has no expectation of return. The return has already been given in the love of Jesus Christ.

Parish leaders, too, exercise good stewardship by consistently reporting how all parish resources are being utilized. A finance council is to be a part of every parish. Its purpose is to advise the pastor and to be in regular dialogue with the pastoral council regarding how contributions are spent, how plant and properties are maintained, and how funds are reserved for future needs.

When parish leaders cannot manage a balanced budget, responsibly pay off past indebtedness, or get more than a few members involved in a variety of ministries, there is most likely a serious stewardship problem.

If a parish is to fulfill its unique mission, its members need to be deeply committed stewards, willing to share their gifts, talents, money, and material resources in the same spirit of generosity as the Lord Jesus Christ, who gave himself for our salvation by his death on the cross.

Ultimately, a sense of stewardship involves the conviction that life is a gift and not simply a product. Believing this means that parishes stand before a mystery that is larger than themselves. They are entrusted with life. They do not own it.

In various ways, then, stewardship in the Church leads people to share in the work of evangelization, in ministries of the word, and in service to persons in need through works of justice and mercy. Evangelization, word, and service are all interrelated with the element of stewardship and vice versa. Together these elements form the community of faith which carries out its call to discipleship.

STEWARDSHIP IN PARISH LIFE

Descriptors

☐ 1. The parish provides opportunities for parishioners to experience their giftedness and to recognize the gratuitous nature of God's blessings.

☐ 2. Formation efforts help parishioners understand their baptismal responsibility to steward their gifts, including the gifts of faith and life in the Church.

☐ 3. Parishioners demonstrate their understanding of Christian stewardship by their willing support of parish and diocesan needs.

☐ 4. The resources of the parish are sufficient to accomplish its mission and the goals and objectives flowing from that mission.

☐ 5. Regular efforts are made to discover parishioners' talents and invite their use in parish service.

☐ 6. Parishioners who offer their gifts in service to the parish mission are given adequate training, encouragement, and supervision.

☐ 7. The parish is not overly dependent on extraordinary fundraisers such as bingo and tickets to support its ordinary budget.

☐ 8. The parish keeps up payments on its debt, if there is one.

☐ 9. Parish facilities are appropriately maintained and adequate for the needs of the parish.

☐ 10. Members of the finance council are persons with interest and experience in budgeting, facilities management, and fundraising and development efforts.

☐ 11. The parish regularly shares a portion of its income with the poor.

ASSESSING STEWARDSHIP IN OUR PARISH

Evidence

(A list of the ways in which our parish currently implements specific items on the checklist)

Example: We tithe 10 percent of our annual parish festival income to support a poor parish in another part of the diocese.

Challenges

(A list of areas that need attention)

Example: We spend most of our council meetings worrying about fundraising.

LEADERSHIP

Effective parish pastoral councils require a shared leadership among clergy and laity which calls forth the gifts of visioning, planning, empowering, and evaluating. These gifts are placed at the service of the community for the fulfillment of the parish mission.

While the pastor bears the ultimate responsibility and authority within a parish, the gifts of the laity "as each one has received" (1 Pt 4:10) are needed and welcomed in the service of the parish as well. Those selected to serve on the parish pastoral council exercise their gifts to vision, plan, empower, and evaluate the parish's programs and initiatives in light of the parish mission.

Although all members of the council are called to leadership, each will carry out that responsibility in a unique way, based on his or her own gifts, talents, and style of leadership. "There are different kinds of spiritual gifts but the same spirit" (1 Cor 12:4). Together, the pastor and council place their gifts at the service of one another and of the parish community. They do so, however, as servants of the Gospel:

> You know that the rulers of the Gentiles lord it over them, and the great ones make their authority over them felt. But it shall not be so among you. Rather, whoever wishes to be great among you shall be your servant; whoever wishes to be first among you shall be your slave. Just so, the Son of Man did not come to be served but to serve and to give his life as a ransom for many. (Matt 20:25-28)

The pastor and council do not work for or under one another, but rather with one another for the Kingdom of God. Together they lead the parish in the ongoing discernment and realization of its mission.

LEADERSHIP IN PARISH LIFE

Descriptors

☐ 1. The pastor, parish staff, and pastoral council according to their appropriate roles share responsibility for visioning, planning, empowering, and evaluating.

☐ 2. The pastoral concerns of the parish are assessed, evaluated, and responded to by the parish pastoral council in collaboration with the pastor and parish staff.

☐ 3. Decisions are made by consensus after a process of discernment, study, and discussion.

☐ 4. Ongoing formation and training of parish leaders is provided for and is informed by diocesan, national and universal church teachings.

☐ 5. Parish leaders delegate responsibility for implementing pastoral activities to competent persons, offering them support, resources, and regular oversight.

☐ 6. Parish personnel are recruited and remunerated according to professional standards and formal job descriptions.

☐ 7. The pastor regularly evaluates parish personnel.

☐ 8. Willingness to share staff with other parishes is considered a viable means of ensuring competency in ministerial leadership.

ASSESSING LEADERSHIP IN OUR PARISH

Evidence

(A list of the ways in which our parish currently implements specific items on the checklist)

Example: We have completed our annual assembly to help assess the needs brought up by parishioners.

Challenges

(A list of areas that need attention)

Example: We do not have job descriptions for our janitor, secretary, or church organist.

Eucharist at the Center

The communal celebration of Sunday Eucharist is both the source and summit of the seven essential elements of parish life. In fact, the goal of every ecclesial activity is that those who share faith and baptism as children of God be united in praising God in the Church, taking part in the eucharistic sacrifice and sharing the Lord's supper. The Eucharist is the center of parish life and of our faith in Christ Jesus. In the Constitution on the Sacred Liturgy from the Second Vatican Council we read:

> Every liturgical celebration, because it is an action of Christ the Priest and of his Body which is the Church, is a sacred action surpassing all others; no other action of the Church can equal its efficacy by the same title and to the same degree.[24]

While many other parish activities enhance the essence of what takes place in the celebration of the Eucharist, none substitute for it. Without the Eucharist at the center of parish life, the parish mission is devoid of meaning and evangelization is without substance because we fail to practice what we preach.

Jesus' command to "Do this in memory of me" (Luke 22:19) is not merely an invitation to imitate what Jesus did. "It is directed at the liturgical celebration, by the apostles and their successors, of the memorial of Christ, of his life, of his death, of his Resurrection, and of his intercession in the presence of the Father. From the beginning the Church has been faithful to the Lord's command."[25]

In the Acts of the Apostles, we read:

> They devoted themselves to the teaching of the apostles and to the communal life, to the breaking of the bread and to the prayers. . . . All who believed were together and had all things in common; they would sell their property and possessions and divide them among all according to each one's need. (Acts 2:42-45)

From the earliest days of the Church, from that first COMMUNITY of faith gathered in WORD and WORSHIP, we receive the mission of EVANGELIZATION, SERVICE, and STEWARDSHIP and the ministry of shared LEADERSHIP. The breaking of the bread in remembrance of Jesus continues to be the font and focal point of parish life.

The seven essential elements of a parish's pastoral life, with the Eucharist at the center, provide the filter through which the new wine is poured into new wineskins. The parish's purpose is constantly sifted through these seven elements as the pastoral council leads the community in the ongoing, prayerful discernment of the call of God to the parish at this moment in time. The pastoral council provides this leadership primarily through the process of pastoral visioning and planning.

III: GUIDE TO PARISH PASTORAL PLANNING

"Would you tell me, please, which way I ought to walk from here?" said Alice.

"That depends a good deal on where you want to get to," said the cat.

"I don't much care where," said Alice.

"Then it doesn't much matter which way you walk," said the cat.

Alice's Adventures in Wonderland
by Lewis Carroll

What Is Pastoral Planning?

Sometimes it seems as if the tail is wagging the dog!

If you don't know where you are going, any road will get you there!

When the fog level rises, we drive more slowly and our horizons shorten!

Without a vision the people perish!

In spite of these warnings about life in general, most people tend to make things up as they go along. And then they wonder why things end up in confusion. Even with a lot of desire, energy, and motivation, without clear direction and vision, a person, a family, an organization and a parish can be all dressed up with nowhere to go.

The planning model in REVISIONING THE PARISH PASTORAL COUNCIL challenges pastoral councils to "make it happen" instead of "let it happen." Pastoral planning is a way of:

- making sure that none of the seven essential elements of parish life is inadvertently overlooked
- ensuring that the future will not come as a thief in the night with the parish unprepared for its coming
- avoiding waste and duplication by modeling good stewardship
- judging the importance and urgency of parish ministries and determining the right order for carrying them out
- deciding what is to be done this year and in the next three to five years
- ensuring that existing parish programs, organizations, and committees are continually evaluated and adjusted to respond to the vision of the parish
- identifying the resources that the parish has and needs
- connecting the mission and goals of the parish to the mission and goals of the diocese
- (finally, and most important) involving the whole parish on a regular basis in the continuing search for a more effective response to God's will.

Pastoral plans can provide a rootedness grounded in the mission of Christ. This is especially important in our world, where the rapid pace of change often gives rise to a sense of fragmentation, even in parish life. A parish pastoral plan becomes a sign of wholeness in a fragmented world.

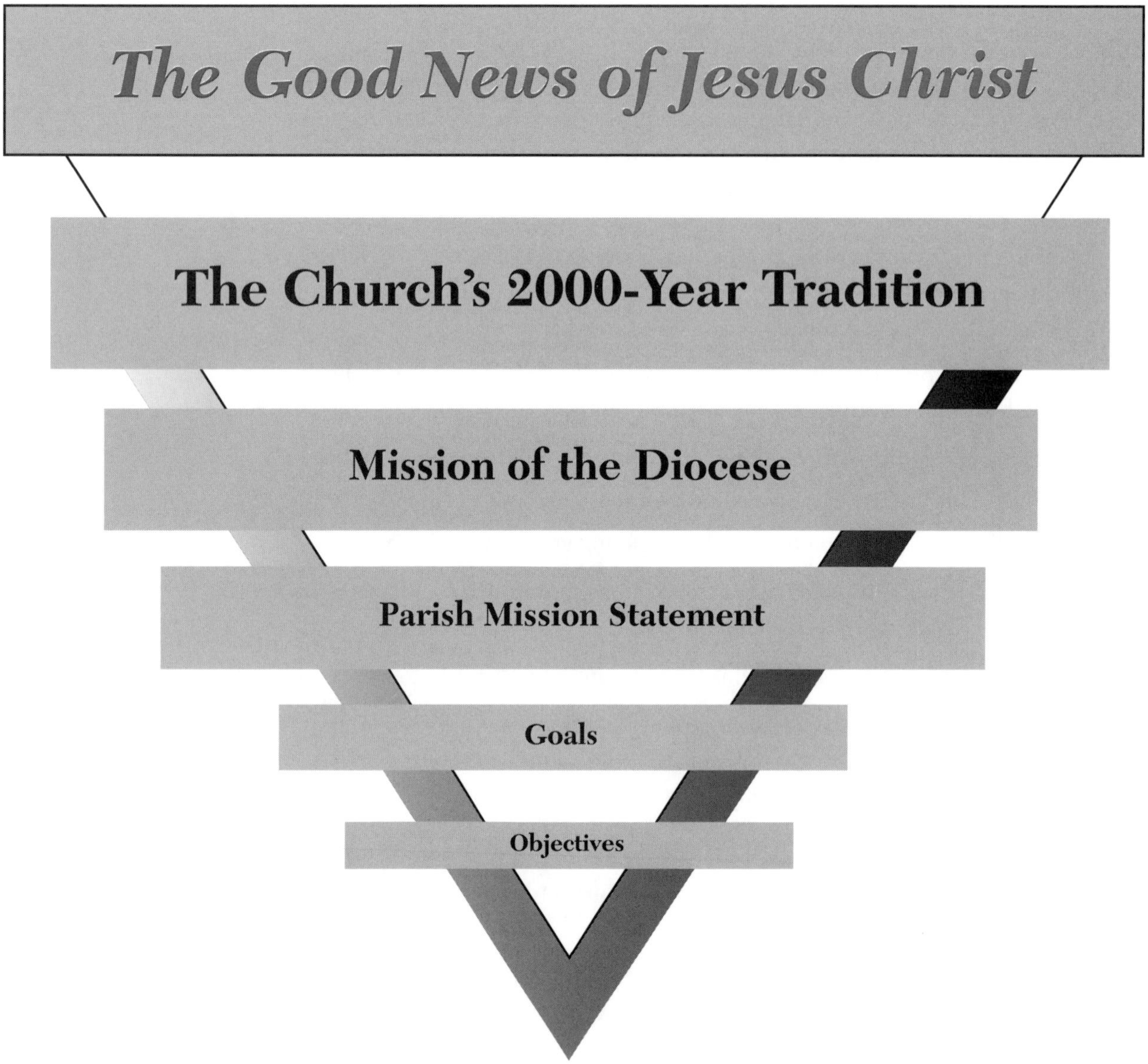
The Good News of Jesus Christ
The Church's 2000-Year Tradition
Mission of the Diocese
Parish Mission Statement
Goals
Objectives

The Components of the Pastoral Plan

A pastoral plan is a "living" document—the unique expression of the mission of a particular parish. The mission of every parish is ultimately grounded in Christ. It is shaped by the two-thousand-year tradition of the Church and flows from the diocesan mission.

The three components of a parish pastoral plan are: (1) the parish mission statement, (2) goals, and (3) objectives.

Component 1—The Mission Statement

Every group needs a definitive mission to survive. Mission statements are not generic nor interchangeable. They are statements of identity and direction describing the present and future. They are philosophical, value-oriented, long-term declarations of fundamental purpose. Mission statements simply say what an organization is trying to do, why it exists. A brief and clear mission statement makes a public declaration about the group's purpose and helps keep priorities in order, build morale, and provide direction for the future.

The mission statement of each parish indicates the unique aspects of its history, tradition, and composition, as well as its particular vision for fulfilling the mission of Jesus Christ. It gives specific expression to the parish intention to live out its calling within the concrete boundaries of its location, resources, and needs. It defines WHY a particular parish exists.

Forming a mission statement involves the processes of discernment and consensus. The pastor and council, having listened to the parish reflect upon its unique characteristics, resources, and gifts, now determine how the parish can best give expression to the diocesan vision and the particular call of God to this parish community.

Component 2—Goals

Goals are descriptive statements of achievements to be attained within three to five years. A goal should be an explicit extension of the mission statement. It ought to be results-oriented, clearly defined, and capable of being supported by related objectives. A goal must be "do-able." The statement of a goal must describe an end point, a specific quantity or quality of outcome to be realized within a given time frame. It should be possible to complete a goal and replace it with a new one. Goals are comprehensive, focusing on the major tasks the group selects for itself.

Goals deal with strengthening existing programs or charting new programs, not merely with continuing existing activities. Goals are statements of WHAT the parish wants to achieve in the coming three to five years.

Component 3—Objectives

Objectives describe concrete, explicit outcomes to be reached in one year in pursuit of a goal. Because objectives are specific and measurable, they are easy to evaluate in terms of both the extent and the quality of achievement attained.

Objectives specify HOW a goal will be achieved by stating what is to be done, who is to do it, and the date by which it is to be completed. By choosing "do-able" and specific objectives, a parish guarantees movement toward a specific goal, eliminating the kinds of nebulous or unending projects which drain energy from even the most faithful parishioners.

THE PARISH PASTORAL PLANNING CYCLE

The primary responsibility of the parish pastoral council is *pastoral planning*. This involves researching, considering, and proposing pastoral goals for the parish community in light of church teaching and the mission of both the local and the larger Church. Once the community has discerned and expressed its mission in light of the seven essential elements, the pastoral council then directs the resources and gifts of the local community toward the fulfillment of that mission. This is accomplished through the process of pastoral planning.

Pastoral planning utilizes effective tools from leadership and management sciences and adds the dimension of prayerful discernment, reflection on gospel values, and awareness of the Church's history and tradition. Through the pastoral planning process, the council discerns what needs to be changed, supported, or enhanced in keeping the parish faithful to its mission. As illustrated in the diagram below, pastoral planning is an ongoing, cyclical process which is always mission-motivated and involves discernment, consensus, goal setting, developing objectives, implementation, and evaluation.

DISCERNMENT

Pastoral planning begins with and is sustained by a process of discernment and assessment. Through prayer, study, and listening, the pastor and council begin to identify and prioritize the ways in which the parish is being called to live out its specific mission.

It cannot be overemphasized how important it is to root the entire process in prayer. Prayer must guide the process of discerning the specific direction that the parish will take. Discernment may be supported by the use of sacred scripture as well as the major church documents, which helps to assure fidelity to the teachings of Christ and the Church.

For more on prayer, refer to the "Prayer" section in Part I.

CONSENSUS

All phases of the pastoral planning cycle utilize the skill of decision-making by consensus. This is a critical element in the transition from parish councils to parish pastoral councils. Consensus is not reached by a majority vote and is not a win/lose situation. Rather, it is a method of decision-making through which a group strives to reach substantial agreement on matters of overall direction and policy which can be supported by all. The council reaches consensus on a matter when all members of the council can live with the decision. This shared ownership of the council's determinations is essential if the council and parish are to be effective in the fulfillment of the mission. Decision-making by consensus gives witness to shared leadership and the building of community which are the most basic parts of parish visioning and mission.

For more on consensus, refer to the "Consensus" section in Part I.

GOAL SETTING

Parish goals are formulated in response to the question, "What will our priorities be for the next few years?" Consideration of other questions may help shed light on what these priorities should be. For example, "Has our reflection on the seven essential elements of parish life pointed to certain areas that need attention?" "What seem to be the greatest needs in our parish?"

After looking at the answers to these or similar questions, and using the information gathered from parishioners, statistical records, local demographics, and other resources, council members deliberate together to reach consensus about parish priorities.

The next step in the pastoral planning process is the development of formal goals, constructive statements that clearly identify areas of challenge and define directions or desired activities.

For more on goal setting, refer to the following section, "Creating a Pastoral Plan."

DEVELOPING OBJECTIVES

Goal setting is followed by the setting of objectives, descriptions of what is to be accomplished within a one-year time frame in working toward a particular goal. At the end of the year, objectives are evaluated, and those that have been successfully implemented are subsequently replaced with new objectives for the following year. If they have not been successfully implemented, they may be repeated or revised for the next year. Objectives are reviewed annually until goals are achieved. Goals, once accomplished, are replaced with new goals. The process of setting, carrying out, and evaluating objectives for these new goals continues the planning process as an integral part of the group's life.

For more on developing objectives, refer to the following section, "Creating a Pastoral Plan."

IMPLEMENTATION

When goals and objectives have been ratified by the parish and publicized to everyone, the council begins the work of inviting people to bring the plan to life. The council's role is empowering and motivating parishioners to offer their time and talents to implement parts of the plan. While it sometimes may be tempting to assign tasks to council or staff members, the effort to find ordinary parishioners with a gift or an interest in a particular goal or objective is essential. Perhaps an existing parish organization or committee can be asked. Stewardship programs reveal people's talents and willingness to serve. Sign-up Sundays, surveys, census records, and simple brainstorming around the council table can surely surface names of those who might be asked to steward the parish mission.

Once in place, implementation groups need supportive oversight to ensure the accomplishment of the objective for which they are responsible. The council can determine its own process for monitoring the implementation, but it should be consistent, helpful, and encouraging. There should be a sense of neither controlling supervision nor indifferent disregard. At the end of the implementation period, those who did the work should be invited to participate in an evaluation process.

For more on implementation and empowerment, refer to the "Empowerment" section in Part IV.

EVALUATION

The evaluation process involves asking such question as "Have we accomplished our objectives?" "What is now being asked of the community in response to the call of God?" "What adjustments, if any, need to be made?" "What are the current challenges?" "To what does the parish need to turn its attention in keeping with its mission?" All such inquiries are part of the evaluation phase, which completes the pastoral planning cycle, leading once again into the discernment phase with an assessment of where the parish needs to go from here.

The pastoral council continually evaluates the parish's goals, objectives, needs, and resources in light of the mission. It engages in ongoing discernment, listening, consensus, and strategizing/goal setting, thus demonstrating the cyclical and continual characteristic of the pastoral planning process.

For more on evaluation, refer to "Follow-up" at the end of the next section on "Creating a Pastoral Plan."

CREATING A PASTORAL PLAN

Preparation: Data Collection

Data gathering offers councils the opportunity to compile factual information about their parish environment and use this information is assessing strengths, weaknesses, needs, and directions. The data should be shared regularly with parishioners and reviewed or updated periodically, if not annually.

Information obtained through data gathering can help give substance to a pastoral plan, making it responsive to the actual situation and not simply to the felt perceptions of a group.

Parish Statistics

Each year the parish submits to the diocese a record of various statistics. It is helpful to review the records of the past five or ten years to see if the parish is growing, declining, maintaining itself, or changing. These records can provide information such as:

- Mass attendance and Mass schedule
- sacramental statistics—baptisms, funerals, confirmations, marriages
- parish census figures—numbers of families, widowed persons, those living alone
- school attendance—Catholic and public
- religious education attendance
- pastoral responsibilities for hospitals, nursing homes, or other facilities
- parish staffing
- liturgical, educational and service ministries
- active parish organizations
- activities and traditions
- fundraising efforts
- parish financial statements
- average giving picture
- budget and indebtedness
- building condition, maintenance costs

Review of Larger Community

Information can be obtained from agencies such as county planning offices, the chamber of commerce, school boards, the telephone company, zoning boards, or regional development offices. Types of information available include:

- total current population of the local area
- population projections
- income and employment statistics
- types and number of housing units
- ethnic information
- total school-age population
- names of civic and service organizations

Other Information

It is also important to identify any ecumenical involvement, inter-parochial collaboration, sharing of resources, or cooperative agreements involving the parish. These could include:

- a deanery youth group
- shared responsibility for a homeless shelter, food pantry, or clothing store
- participation in interfaith worship and service projects
- combined religious education programs involving two or more parishes
- shared parish staff, such as a parish social minister or evangelization director
- coordinated training for liturgical ministries

QUESTIONS TO HELP DEFINE A PARISH MISSION STATEMENT

(To be used at a parish assembly or other parish consultation)

If Jesus were here today, what words would he give us to direct our future?

Why do you think the universal Catholic Church exists?

What makes our parish unique and special?

HELPFUL HINTS FOR WRITING A CLEAR MISSION STATEMENT

I. Identity:

In general, this part of the mission statement indicates the elements which identify the parish—its name, location, history, make-up, unique character, etc.

Samples:
We, the parish community of...
Continuing in the tradition of...

II. Purpose:

Speaks to the values, beliefs, central focus, reason for the existence of the parish.

Samples:
We are a parish which values, believes, etc....
Our mission is to...

III. Function:

Identifies the "to whom" and "what" of the life of the parish in broad categories.

Samples:
We are committed to...
Our commitments include...

IV. Future:

Addresses areas of challenge, elements that are missing or in need of strengthening

Samples:
We seek to become...
We are called to...

What to Ask in Evaluating an Existing Mission Statement

1. How old is the mission statement?

2. The what degree was the parish community involved in shaping this statement?

3. How much does it influence current parish life?

4. Does it reflect the four key areas of Identity, Purpose, Function, Future?

5. Is it in keeping with the diocesan vision and the seven essential elements?

6. Are our present strengths and needs reflected in it?

7. Does it still inspire as the foundation of the pastoral plan of the parish?

8. Would our parish profit by "revisiting" the process for mission statements, allowing the present council to revise the mission statement to more accurately reflect the current reality of our parish?

A Closer Look at Writing Goals and Objectives

QUESTIONS TO HELP DETERMINE GOALS AND OBJECTIVES

(To be used at a parish assembly or other parish consultation)

What do I as a member expect of my parish?

How should we reach out to the broader community from our parish?

What do our demographics and data suggest that we do for the future?

Which of the seven elements do we need to focus on and why?

HELPFUL HINTS FOR WRITING GOALS

What Is a Goal?

A goal is a brief, clear statement of an outcome to be reached within three to five years. It is a broad, general description that sets forth not how something is to be done, but rather what the results will look like.

In pastoral planning, a goal is directly related to one of the seven essential elements. In addition, it must flow from the diocesan and parish mission statements.

What Are the Parts of a Goal?

An active verb: Choose a verb that truly describes the movement which you are projecting for the parish. Do you plan to strengthen something already in existence or begin something new? Will you establish, renovate, create, institute, implement, or expand a project or program? Be sure the verb expresses it clearly.

A description of what you will do: Be succinct in naming what it is you plan to do in approximately three to five years. It is not necessary to add many details; keep what you say brief.

Some indication of quantity or quality: Expand the basic description enough so that you know how much of the outcome and/or the quality of the outcome you want to see.

Criteria for a Well-written Goal

- Is the goal realistic?
- Is the goal challenging and long-range?
- Does the goal clearly present just one central outcome to be achieved?

Some examples of goals:

1. To develop responsible lay leadership in the parish by encouraging all members to share their gifts.
2. To enrich our worship life through expanded prayer opportunities in the parish.
3. To restructure parish religious education efforts for children of post-initiation age.
4. To deepen our own faith in the Good News of Jesus Christ in order to bring it to those who are no longer active in the Church.
5. To establish neighborhood faith communities in at least one-third of the parish.

Worksheet on Goals

This goal is related to the essential element of ______________________________.

To ____________________ ____.

(active verb) (a description of what you would like to see in three to five years)

____

(expansion of the basic description to indicate how much of the outcome and/or the quality of the outcome you want to see)

CRITERIA FOR A WELL-WRITTEN GOAL

1. Does this goal flow directly from the parish and diocesan mission statements? ___ Y ___ N

2. Is the goal realistic? ___ Y ___ N

3. Is the goal challenging and long-range? ___ Y ___ N

4. Does the goal clearly present just one central outcome to be achieved? ___ Y ___ N

Sample Worksheet on Goals

This goal is related to the essential element of ___***Evangelization***___.

To ___***create***___ ___***a spirit of hospitality***___.

(active verb) (a description of what you would like to see in three to five years)

___***in all "total parish events," i.e., Sunday Mass and socials***___

(expansion of the basic description to indicate how much of the outcome and/or the quality of the outcome you want to see)

Criteria for a Well-written Goal

1. Does this goal flow directly from the parish and diocesan mission statements? _✓_ Y ___ N

2. Is the goal realistic? _✓_ Y ___ N

3. Is the goal challenging and long-range? _✓_ Y ___ N

4. Does the goal clearly present just one central outcome to be achieved? _✓_ Y ___ N

HELPFUL HINTS FOR WRITING OBJECTIVES

What Is an Objective?

An objective is a brief, clear statement of an outcome to be reached within one year as a step toward one goal in the parish pastoral plan. An objective is specific about what will be done and who will be affected. The outcome is stated in terms that are quantifiable and measurable and each objective specifies a completion date.

What Are the Parts of an Objective?

An action verb: Be very careful to use a verb that indicates what you plan to do. Are you going to study, to initiate, to plan, to start, to design, to assess, to invite, to offer, to create, to use, to research?

A *specific task to be completed:* State "what" will be accomplished in order to move closer to fulfilling the larger goal.

A *target group:* The people to be reached should be identified (directly or indirectly).

A *completion date:* Name the date by which you expect the task to be done, normally within one year.

Other Considerations

In formulating the objective, it is helpful during the planning process to identify some practical matters related to the accomplishment of that objective.

> *Major tasks involved:* List briefly what steps will have to be taken to achieve the objective. It may be helpful to draw up a timeline.
>
> *Costs involved:* Estimate what expenses or resources will be needed to accomplish the objective.
>
> *Persons involved:* Identify persons or groups who may be affected by this objective and/or need to be involved in carrying it out.

Worksheet on Objectives

This objective is related to Goal ____.

(identify by name or number)

To ____________________ ____.

(active verb) *(qualified outcome of action specified here)*

by ______/ ______ / ______.

(deadline date not more than a year away)

Major tasks needed to achieve this objective:

Costs likely to be incurred and estimated amounts:

Who (persons or groups) will be most affected by this objective and/or need to be involved in carrying it out?

CRITERIA FOR A WELL-WRITTEN OBJECTIVE

Does the objective include the following?

- An action verb ___ Y ___ N
- A specific "what" ___ Y ___ N
- A target group to be reached (stated or implied) ___ Y ___ N
- A date by which the objective will be accomplished ___ Y ___ N

Sample Worksheet on Objectives

This objective is related to Goal ***on Hospitality***.

(identify by name or number)

To ***develop*** (*active verb*) ***ten family teams of greeters for weekend liturgies*** (*specific outcome of action*).

by ***June*** / ***30*** / ***2001***.

(deadline date not more than a year away)

Major tasks needed to achieve this objective:

- ***explain to parishioners***
- ***identify families (volunteers and invited)***
- ***sponsor training session(s)***
- ***create schedule***

Costs likely to be incurred and estimated amounts:

- ***books for training session—$5.95 per family***
- ***speaker—$50 stipend***
- ***permanent name tags—$3.95 per person***
- ***printing and mailing schedules—$20 a year***

Who (persons or groups) will be most affected by this objective and/or need to be involved in carrying it out?

- ***Task Force on Family Life***
- ***Liturgy Coordinator***
- ***Ushers***

Criteria for a Well-written Objective

Does the objective include the following?

- An action verb ✓ Y ___ N
- A specific "what" ✓ Y ___ N
- A target group to be reached (stated or implied) ✓ Y ___ N
- A date by which the objective will be accomplished ✓ Y ___ N

Practice in Working with Goals and Objectives

SOME SAMPLE GOALS AND OBJECTIVES

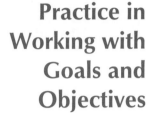

GOAL: To develop responsible lay leadership in the parish by encouraging all members to share their gifts.

OBJECTIVES:

1. To involve ten pastoral council members in two day-long workshops on Vatican II theology and leadership skills by / / .
2. To sponsor a time and talent fair in conjunction with annual stewardship drive by / / .
3. To offer a day of reflection/workshop for leaders of all parish organizations by / / .

GOAL: To enrich our worship life through expanded prayer opportunities in the parish.

OBJECTIVES:

1. To introduce the practice of Morning Prayer on days when there is no daily Mass by Advent / / .
2. To recruit and develop leaders for Liturgy of the Word with Children by / / .
3. To sponsor two twelve-hour family retreats for at least ten families each time by / / .

GOAL: To restructure parish religious formation efforts for children of post-initiation age.

OBJECTIVES:

1. To consult with diocesan catechetical resource persons concerning programs and materials by / / .
2. To collaborate with two nearby parishes to employ a professional coordinator of religious formation for our parishes by / / .
3. To offer four family-based programs on the Creed by / / .

GOAL: To deepen our own faith in the Good News of Jesus Christ in order to bring it to those who are no longer active in the Church.

OBJECTIVES:

1. To train four teams of two to be scripture discussion group leaders by / / .
2. To introduce the parish to information about the new evangelization by / / .
3. To plan a parish renewal (to occur during Lent next year) by / / .

GOAL: To establish neighborhood faith communities in at least one-third of the parish.

OBJECTIVES:

1. To create a parish grid of streets and census data by / / .
2. To offer three information sessions on neighborhood faith communities for interested parishioners by / / .
3. To research available training materials on small Christian communities by / / .

Samples of Weak Goals

Review the following goals and see if you can identify their weaknesses. Answers appear on the next page.

1. To find out what the needs of the parish are spiritually, socially, ministerially, and educationally.

2. To pursue the completion of various issues which have been raised by parishioners in the past three years.

3. To recognize that our parish is comprised of many unique individuals and families coming together as one to celebrate our Catholic faith.

4. To stimulate an educational program designed to improve our understanding of the faith.

5. More meaningful worship.

6. To see that every member of the parish who lives alone is checked on at least once a day.

DISCUSSION OF WEAK GOALS

1. To find out what the needs of the parish are spiritually, socially, ministerially, and educationally.

   This may be a goal of the parish pastoral council as it begins to develop a parish plan, but it is merely a part of data collection and/or a parish assembly. Thus, it should not be listed as a parish-wide goal.

2. To pursue the completion of various issues which have been raised by parishioners in the past three years.

   This is so broad and general as to be unmeasurable. At the end of three to five years, how would the parish know it had accomplished this goal? It would be better to begin with one of the "various issues" which seem to be important to parish life and develop a goal around it.

3. To recognize that our parish is comprised of many unique individuals and families coming together as one to celebrate our Catholic Faith.

   This statement asks that the parish "recognize" a certain fact, but it does not really speak to what the goal is about. Is this goal about family life, about unity in the parish, about worship, or about the transmission of the faith? A goal needs to have one clear focus.

4. To stimulate an educational program designed to improve our understanding of the faith.

   To what does the verb "stimulate" apply? One can stimulate persons, or one can propose, plan, implement, or evaluate a program. Is not the purpose of most educational programs in the church to improve our understanding of the faith? What is this group really seeking? A more exciting, stimulating program? It is very important to think about the verb and the real issue at hand.

5. More meaningful worship.

   This goal is so broad as to be impossible to accomplish. Meaningful to whom? In what way? What action is desired here? It is important to state precisely what it is that will be accomplished in three to five years, and to state it in such a way that achievement of the goals can be demonstrated with concrete evidence.

6. To see that every member of the parish who lives alone is checked on at least once a day.

   This is actually more like an objective; it is very specific and can probably be done in less than one year. Perhaps there was an overarching goal and this was one part of it. For example, "To extend the care and concern of the parish community to those who are most in need." Those who live alone are one such group. Other objectives could address the poor or single parents or the disabled.

Samples of Weak Objectives

Review the following objectives and see if you can identify their weaknesses. Perhaps you can attempt re-writing them! (Answers appear on the next page.)

GOAL: To enhance the understanding and celebration of the Eucharist in our parish.

OBJECTIVE:

A mission on the Eucharist.

GOAL: To promote a sense of family and belonging.

OBJECTIVE:

To build on a parish community; Welcome Wagon; home visits; To promote human dignity, family values, and unity.

GOAL: To increase the amount of church and community outreach.

OBJECTIVE:

Outreach to fallen-away parishioners.

GOAL: To enrich our parish worship life by increasing participation in the prayer opportunities which are provided.

OBJECTIVE:

To form a committee that will investigate our music program and subsequently establish an enhanced direction for it.

DISCUSSION OF WEAK OBJECTIVES

GOAL: To enhance the understanding and celebration of the Eucharist in our parish.

OBJECTIVE:

A mission on the Eucharist.

What action is planned here? Will the mission be planned this year? Offered this year? When? An objective needs to have specific measurable tasks and a timeline. Again, the verb is critical.

Suggested strengthened objective: To plan and offer during Lent of _______ a parish mission focused on the Eucharist.

GOAL: To promote a sense of family and belonging.

OBJECTIVE:

To build on a parish community; Welcome Wagon; home visits; to promote human dignity, family values, and unity.

These are ideas for objectives, but they are not articulated in a way that leads to clear, measurable action. What does it mean to build on a parish community? How will the parish promote human dignity? Who will be visited? Is the parish collaborating with the existing Welcome Wagon group or is it setting up a new church group? Objectives must have *one* clear outcome and timeline. What, who, when?

Suggested strengthened objective: By January _____ , to create a parish welcome packet to be distributed to all newcomers registering in the parish. (In the future this objective could grow into personal delivery of the packet through home visits done by a parish group.)

GOAL: To increase the amount of church and community outreach.

OBJECTIVE:

Outreach to fallen-away parishioners.

This objective is not specific enough. What is needed here is a verb, "to research resources on, to plan, to initiate, to expand efforts at."

Also needed are measurable limits, such as "10 percent of registered inactive parishioners," or "through a phone survey to every inactive household." Finally, the statement should include a date by which the action is to be accomplished and an evaluation can be made to determine whether the objective was met. it needs a time limit, so that an evaluation can identify whether or not the objective was met.

Suggested strengthened objectives:

- To research available materials to use with inactive Catholics by / / .
- To select one approach for the parish to use in outreach efforts to inactive Catholics by / / .
- To train twenty-five parishioners in how to use the evangelization materials selected for outreach efforts by / / .

GOAL: To enrich our parish worship life by increasing participation in the prayer opportunities provided.

OBJECTIVE:

To form a committee that will investigate our music program and subsequently establish an enhanced direction for it.

What will really be done here and on what timeline? When will the committee be formed? What kind of investigation will it do? Will the committee make decisions or merely make recommendations? How will this council know when the objective has been achieved?

Suggested strengthened objective: To authorize a committee to review our music program and make recommendations to the pastor, council, and parish staff about enhancing it by / / .

Follow-up: Evaluation

An evaluation at the end of each implementation period is essential. Even though a project may have been completed, it is important for those responsible for it to have the opportunity to bring closure to the process.

Ongoing oversight no doubt keeps the council aware of progress and any difficulties encountered by the implementation group, but a final "amen" helps with a review of the entire endeavor. Although verbal reports may be adequate in certain instances, a final written summary is more beneficial. It helps implementers share their experience, do some analysis of what was effective and what was not, and, most important, indicate future directions. Those involved with a particular initiative are asked for their best advice about what needs to happen next. This step not only recognizes the work of the implementation team, but also respects its experience and ability to offer reality-based suggestions for moving closer to the goal.

Finally, if the recorder is able to garner evaluation reports from each implementation group, these reports may be kept as part of the annual record. The experience and the accomplishment of the group can serve as both a historical and a practical reference point. The collective wisdom provides inspiration and advice for new implementation groups. Also, councils can consult the record as they determine new goals and objectives in their ongoing development of the pastoral plan.

A celebration of accomplishment is important. While most workers in the parish do not seek public recognition for themselves, all can enter into a feeling of parish pride as together they help move the parish along in its plan for growth and vitality. Don't omit this very important final phase of evaluation and closure on each year's objectives.

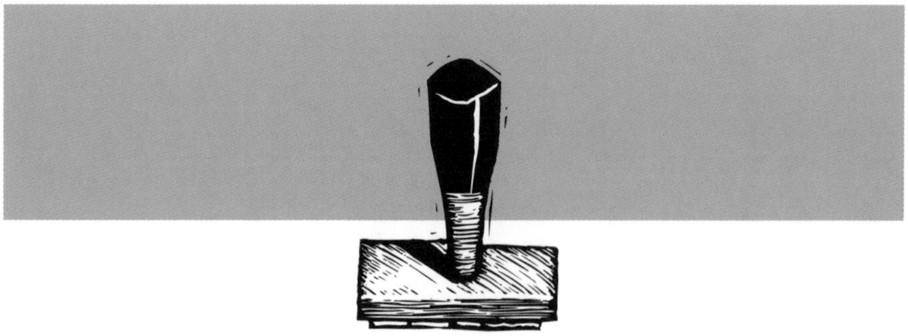

Evaluation Worksheet

GOAL:

OBJECTIVE:

1. Describe how well this objective was accomplished. What was done?

2. What was especially helpful in getting the objective accomplished?

3. What, if anything, got in the way or hindered progress in reaching the objective?

4. In light of the above, what suggestions do you have for follow-up or building on this objective?

Sample Evaluation Worksheet

GOAL: ***To create a spirit of hospitality at all "total parish events."***

OBJECTIVE: ***To develop ten family teams of greeters for weekend liturgies by / / .***

1. Describe how well this objective was accomplished. What was done?

We presently have twelve family teams who rotate at three Masses on weekends, with two families at each Mass. Five families volunteered right away—we had to dig to find the rest. The training session was excellent. Mr. Johnson was dynamic speaker and he could talk about his own experience of greeters in his parish. Our parishioners seem to appreciate efforts, and families like doing the ministry.

2. What was especially helpful in getting the objective accomplished?

- ***Explanation at Sunday Mass was clear and inviting.***
- ***Enthusiasm of families.***
- ***Organizational style of liturgy coordinator.***

3. What, if anything, got in the way or hindered progress in reaching the objective?

- ***At first we looked only for families with children but later realized that older couples whose children were grown were also very effective and dependable.***
- ***Ushers did not attend planning session and consequently we had to go back and work with them on their continuing role.***
- ***Timeline was too short; we didn't have greeters in place until Advent.***

4. In light of the above, what suggestions do you have for follow-up or building on this objective?

- ***Having coffee and donuts after some Masses***
- ***We need some way of following up with newcomers or occasional worshipers***
- ***How about taking Communion to the sick? (We miss you and you are part of our parish.)***
- ***Recruit some new families to add to the group.***

Two Samples of Three-Year Plans

Here are two examples of how a pastoral plan might grow over a three-year cycle. Note that goals remain the same, but objectives build on previous work.

PARISH A

SAMPLE PARISH PASTORAL PLAN 1997-1998
(Developed during the spring of 1997)

GOAL I:
To establish religious formation opportunities for parishioners of all ages.
(RELATED TO ELEMENT OF WORD)

Objective 1: To evaluate current catechesis for children by January 1998.
Objective 2: To research available materials and processes for children's catechesis by April 1998.
Objective 3: To explore with other parishes in the area the feasibility of beginning junior high youth ministry by January 1998.
Objective 4: To host one event for junior high youth and invite youth from other parishes to participate by May 1998.
Objective 5: To develop a program for parents of elementary children on their role as primary religious educators by May 1998.
Objective 6: To plan and offer an adult Bible study during Lent 1998.

GOAL II:
To enhance the celebration of Sunday Eucharist
(RELATED TO ELEMENT OF WORSHIP)

Objective 1: To invite the diocesan Worship office to visit our parish and assess the present celebration of the Sunday Eucharist by October 1997.
Objective 2: To initiate the role of cantors by Lent 1998.
Objective 3: To provide "refresher" training for those who are presently servers, ushers, lectors, and eucharistic ministers by March 1998.
Objective 4: To recruit new liturgical ministers on Pentecost 1998.

GOAL III:
To establish public outreach efforts in the local community
(RELATED TO ELEMENT OF SERVICE)

Objective 1: To survey service opportunities already in existence in the area by January 1998.
Objective 2: To determine which parishioners are already assisting with both civic and ecumenical social outreach projects by January 1998.
Objective 3: To plan and provide a forum for parish study of the U.S. bishops' document, *Communities of Salt and Light,* by April 1998.
Objective 4: To decide what involvements would be appropriate future service opportunities for our parish by May 1998.

***SAMPLE PARISH PASTORAL PLAN* 1998-1999**
(Developed during the spring of 1998)

GOAL I:
To establish religious formation opportunities for parishioners of all ages.
(RELATED TO ELEMENT OF WORD)

Objective 1: To offer a series of six sessions for parents of elementary children on "Parenting the Faith of Children" by May 1999.
Objective 2: To plan and offer two intergenerational "Family Formation Days" in November 1998 and February 1999.
Objective 3: To study and revise the post-initiation programs for children between third and sixth grades by May 1999.
Objective 4: To convene a junior high team (youth and adults) to serve with others who are organizing junior high youth ministry in the area by October 1998.
Objective 5: To expand adult Bible Study to include the Advent and Lenten seasons during 1998-1999.
Objective 6: To plan a total parish renewal project for the Millennium (to be held in fall 2000) by June 1999.

GOAL II:
To enhance the celebration of Sunday Eucharist
(RELATED TO ELEMENT OF WORSHIP)

Objective 1: To plan and offer a retreat/workshop for all liturgical ministers by Advent 1998.
Objective 2: To hire a part-time music coordinator to work with cantors and the choir by June 1999.
Objective 3: To educate parishioners on a basic understanding of Eucharist throughout Ordinary Time during 1998-99.

GOAL III:
To establish public outreach efforts in the local community
(RELATED TO ELEMENT OF SERVICE)

Objective 1: To publicize existing service commitments by parishioners and possible opportunities in our area by October 1998.
Objective 2: To organize a "response team" to work with the St. Vincent de Paul store in meeting emergencies in our area by September 1998.
Objective 3: To support through special collections the work of the local food bank and the interfaith shelter, beginning monthly in July 1998.
Objective 4: To organize and hold a program on "The Everyday Face of Violence" by June 1999.

***SAMPLE PARISH PASTORAL PLAN* 1999-2000**
(Developed during the spring of 1999)

GOAL I:
To establish religious formation opportunities for parishioners of all ages.
(RELATED TO ELEMENT OF WORD)

Objective 1: To offer a series of four sessions for parents of junior high children on "Keeping Our Kids Catholic" by May 2000.
Objective 2: To plan and offer four intergenerational "Family Formation Days" by June 2000.
Objective 3: To initiate and evaluate a new program of religious formation for third through sixth graders by May 2000.
Objective 4: To train two leaders and introduce the Catechesis of the Good Shepherd for pre-school children by September 1999.
Objective 5: To hire a qualified director of religious formation in collaboration with two neighboring parishes by June 2000.

Goal II:
To enhance the celebration of Sunday Eucharist
(RELATED TO ELEMENT OF WORSHIP)

Objective 1: To sponsor with other parishes in the region a music workshop for developing choirs and cantors by December 1999.
Objective 2: To offer Evening Prayer on Sundays in Advent and Lent of 1999-2000.
Objective 3: To develop details of parish renewal project "The Day of the Lord" and begin publicity to the parish by January 2000.

Goal III:
To establish public outreach efforts in the local community
(RELATED TO ELEMENT OF SERVICE)

Objective 1: To explore adopting a refugee family, and if feasible to begin that process by January 2000.
Objective 2: To initiate and plan with appropriate local organizations a Millennium "Jubilee" rally for July 4, 2000.
Objective 3: To recruit and train ten parishioners (teens and adults) to work at the food bank on the first Saturday of each month beginning July 1999.
Objective 4: To plan and offer three educational sessions with other churches in town on "Breaking the Chain of Violence" by June 2000.

PARISH B

SAMPLE PASTORAL PLAN 1997-98
(Developed during the spring of 1997)

GOAL I:
To increase by 25 percent the members of our faith family who participate in the ministries and activities of our parish
(RELATED TO ELEMENT OF STEWARDSHIP)

Objective 1: To recruit at least twelve parishioners as greeters for the Sunday Eucharist by Ash Wednesday 1998.
Objective 2: To develop a parish directory (names, addresses, telephone numbers) by April 1, 1998.
Objective 3: To revitalize the liturgical ministries (music, lector, server, eucharistic minister) by holding a training workshop before June 30, 1998.

GOAL II:
To introduce a program of outreach to the inactive of our parish
(RELATED TO ELEMENT OF EVANGELIZATION)

Objective 1: To develop systems of communication with the shut-ins of our parish by March 31, 1998.
Objective 2: To identify the inactive of our parish by January 1, 1998.
Objective 3: To survey the inactive of our parish to obtain the reason for their lack of participation by June 30, 1998.

GOAL III:
To enrich the personal and communal prayer life of our parishioners
(RELATED TO ELEMENT OF WORSHIP)

Objective 1: To plan and offer a parish mission relating to prayer by June 30, 1998.
Objective 2: To offer a video series on prayer to the parishioners by December 1997.

SAMPLE PASTORAL PLAN 1998-99
(Developed during the spring of 1998)

GOAL I:
To increase by 25 percent the members of our faith family who participate in the ministries and activities of our parish
(RELATED TO ELEMENT OF STEWARDSHIP)

Objective 1: To complete a time and talent survey of parishioners by March 31, 1999.
Objective 2: To publish a directory of parish organizations and ministry groups by December 31, 1998.
Objective 3: To sponsor a retreat and workshop day for liturgical ministers by June 30, 1999.

GOAL II:
To introduce a program of outreach to the inactive of our parish
(RELATED TO ELEMENT OF EVANGELIZATION)

Objective 1: To initiate parish visitors to the homebound by Christmas, 1999.
Objective 2: To mail information and invitations to all parish activities to inactive parishioners on a monthly basis, beginning September 1999.

GOAL III:
To enrich the personal and communal prayer life of our parishioners
(RELATED TO ELEMENT OF WORSHIP)

Objective 1: To begin a monthly study group on prayer by September 30, 1998.
Objective 2: To educate parishioners about different kinds of prayer beginning in Advent, 1998.
Objective 3: To offer Evening Prayer on a seasonal basis by June 30, 1999.

SAMPLE PASTORAL PLAN 1999-2000
(Developed during the spring of 1999)

GOAL I:
To increase by 25 percent the members of our faith family who participate in the ministries and activities of our parish
(RELATED TO ELEMENT OF *STEWARDSHIP*)

Objective 1: To plan and carry out one intergenerational program for adults and children by Easter 2000.
Objective 2: To add one new person to every organization, committee, and ministry group between July 1, 1999 and June 30, 2000.

GOAL II:
To introduce a program of outreach to the inactive of our parish
(RELATED TO ELEMENT OF *EVANGELIZATION*)

Objective 1: To recruit and prepare eucharistic ministers to the homebound, and begin this ministry on Easter 2000.
Objective 2: To plan and hold a "Come and See" evening for inactive parishioners by December 31, 1999.

GOAL III:
To enrich the personal and communal prayer life of our parishioners
(RELATED TO ELEMENT OF *WORSHIP*)

Objective 1: To plan and offer a novena in preparation for Pentecost 2000.
Objective 2: To sponsor an interfaith day of prayer for World Peace for the people of the region during January 2000.

PARISH INVESTMENT IN THE PARISH PASTORAL PLAN

START-UP PROCESS FOR PASTORAL PLANNING

The primary task of the parish pastoral council is pastoral planning. The planning process involves identifying and prioritizing the ways in which the parish is being called to live out its specific mission.

The pastoral council needs to devise an appropriate way to engage the entire parish in this process. This could occur through a series of convenings, such as parish assemblies or various forms of listening sessions. Surveys or questionnaires distributed at weekend liturgies or by mail are another means of eliciting parishioners' expressions of their hopes and aspirations.

The seven essential elements provide both a context and a format for the process. Used as a framework, they help to ensure that the focus is always on the pastoral mission and the process does not deteriorate into complaining, blaming, or wasting time and energy on peripheral issues. The importance of engaging significant numbers of parishioners in this part of the planning process guarantees fuller participation in and ownership of the parish pastoral plan.

Here is a suggested startup process for parish pastoral planning.

1. Parish pastoral council establishes a timeline and schedules dates on parish calendar
   Council develops communication/publicity plan
   Data gathering (statistics, history, etc.) begins

2. Council prepares parish for assemblies through active publicity plan, invitations to key people
   Data gathering continues
   Preparation of informational presentations, handouts, name tags, etc.

3. First Parish Assembly—to gather ideas for mission statement/goals
   Collation of ideas generated at assembly

4. Council drafts mission statement/goals using ideas from Assembly I
   Council plans communication/ratification of mission statement/goals
   Council plans "Goal Sign-up" Sunday

5. Council refines the publicity plan to be sure "Sign-up" Sunday is effective
   Council plans and prepares Second Assembly

6. Council checks the sign-ups to be sure all goals are covered, invites key people to attend
   Second Parish Assembly—to ratify mission statement and to brainstorm objectives

7. Council collates all ideas and establishes objectives for year
   Council determines implementation groups and delegates objectives
   Plan (mission statement, goals, objectives) presented to parish and diocese

It is important to keep the momentum going. If the process is too quick, there is time neither for the parishioners to absorb what is happening nor for the council to do thorough preparation for the various parts. If the process is dragged out over too long a period, both council and parishioners lose interest.

Parts 1 and 2 take approximately six weeks and culminate in the First Assembly.

Parts 3, 4, 5, and 6 take approximately six weeks and culminate in the Second Assembly.

Part 7 takes approximately one month.

GENERATING THE PARISH PASTORAL PLAN

This chart demonstrates the "back and forth" rhythm between the work of the council itself and the opportunities the council provides for the parish at large to become invested in the plan.

PARISH PASTORAL COUNCIL	PARISH AT LARGE
Develops communication plan • seven elements • planning process • invitation to Assembly I **Prepares Assembly I** **Gathers data and prepares data report**	
	Participates in Assembly I • history • prayer and discernment • response to questions
Prepares a draft mission statement • collates Assembly I data • drafts mission statement **Determines areas of goals** • limits scope of goals • drafts goals **Coordinates Goal Sign-up Sunday**	
	Participates in Goal Sign-up Sunday
Prepares Assembly II	
	Participates in Assembly II • ratifies mission statement • ratifies goals • works in goal sub-groups to brainstorm objectives
Prepares Parish Pastoral Plan • gathers Assembly II ideas • organizes, edits ideas into objectives • determines implementation plan • presents completed pastoral plan to • parish and diocese	

Planning the First Assembly of the Start-up Process

An example of how one parish adapted the idea of the parish assembly

Publicity Group *(Members of the council)*
Implemented a four-week council plan for getting interest stirred up in the parish

- Pulpit talks by council members
- Bulletins, bulletin boards, flyers, etc.
- Phone committee to call parishioners
- Attractive invitation mailed to all registered parishioners
- Council members stationed at doors of church after every Mass
- Free admission tickets (to the future of our parish) on last Sunday before assembly

History Group *(Members of the council and other interested parishioners)*
Prepared oral and display history of parish

- Gathered pictures, letters, significant bulletins, booklets
- Arranged a history display with lots of photos
- Planned and practiced the telling of the parish story

Data Collection Group *(Members of the council and other appropriate parishioners)*
Compiled basic data to present at assembly

- Parish statistics on membership, sacraments, Mass attendance, etc.
- General information on demographics of parish
- Parish material assets and liabilities: condition of property, debts, etc.
- Decision on presentation method (oral and/or written) and person(s) responsible

Prayer and Process Group *(Members of the council)*
Organized the assembly's content, schedule, procedures

- Established agenda, schedule
- Planned prayer experience
- Designated the leader for the assembly
- Prepared all materials needed for assembly

Hospitality Group *(Members of the council and appropriate parishioners)*
Made arrangements for physical details of assembly

- Talked with prayer/process group about needed set-ups, microphone, etc.
- Set up the room with tables for group discussion, history display, etc.
- Arranged for refreshments
- Recruited teens to be greeters and "runners" for passing out and collecting materials.

THE FIRST ASSEMBLY

An example of one parish assembly schedule

6:00 All council members, pastor, staff, greeters and hospitality committee arrived, wore distinctive name tags, and reviewed all details for the evening.

6:30 Gathering time: people arrived, registered, received name tags, prayer papers.

Time for viewing the history display.

6:55 Leader encouraged people to sit at tables and to fill in empty spaces.

7:00 The assembly started on time!
Pastor gave warm welcome, introduced the leader for the evening.

7:10 Leader introduced history group, which made its presentation.

Leader invited and facilitated the storytelling of parishioners, especially the "elders."

7:20 Leader gave overview of the assembly, including information about its purpose and where it fits in the planning process.

7:25 Prayer led by prayer planners.
(It consisted of a hymn, prayer, scripture reading, a sharing question, petitions, Our Father.)

7:35 Leader introduced the first three questions which would shape the mission statement. Each question was on a separate color-coded card and had a brief "lead in" by a council member to stimulate the thinking of the group. After allowing two minutes for written responses (silence), the leader asked people to share their responses with others at their table for another two to three minutes. Then one person from each table reported to the whole group on ONE idea that came up at their table. All the cards were collected and the next one distributed.

These first three questions were:

1. ***If Jesus were here today, what words would he give us to direct our future?***

2. ***Why do you think the universal Catholic Church exists?***

3. ***What makes our parish unique and special?***

8:00 Break

8:10 Leader began calling back the group.

8:15 Data group presented summary of statistics, verbally and with a simple handout.

8:20 Leader asked questions 4–6, again providing a lead-in to each one. Used the same procedure as above, i.e., individual writing, table discussion, table report.

4. What do I as a member expect of my parish?

5. How should we reach out to the broader community from our parish?

6. What do our demographics and data suggest that we do for the future?

8:35 A council member reviewed seven essential elements, using the a large illustration of the diagram on page 62.

(Note: this is not the occasion for first-time teaching! Parishioners should have heard about the essential elements before this!)

8:40 Leader asked question 7.

7. Which of the seven essential elements do we need to focus on and why?

8:45 Leader concluded by:

- summarizing the evening
- explaining the next step (council writing draft of mission statement and goals using what the people had said)
- promising continuing communication
- offering thanks for attendance that evening
- extending invitation to the next assembly, giving date and time

8:55 Pastor added his thanks, hopes, and blessing to all.

Goal Sign-up Sunday

Publicity

Between the first and second assemblies intense publicity is needed, both on the mission statement and goals. At no time should parishioners wonder about the sources of these documents.

Pre-registration

The idea of Sign-up Sunday is to get commitments from parishioners in contributing to the development of the objectives of the parish plan. Without an investment in the plan, implementation will be difficult, if not impossible.

Process

Copies of the mission statement and the goals (numbered for easy identification) are distributed to everyone at Mass, along with a card on which parishioners can indicate that they will attend the meeting and note which goal they are interested in. If they cannot attend the meeting, they have the option of noting that they are willing to help with a particular goal.

Here is a sample of the sign-up card:

_____ I will attend the Parish Assembly scheduled on Thursday, __/__/__ from 7 to 9 P.M. At the assembly I am interested in contributing my ideas to GOAL ________.
(number)

_____ I am unable to attend the Parish Assembly but I am interested in working on GOAL ________.
(number)

______________________________ ______________
(name) *(phone)*

Sign-up

During the Sunday liturgy, the mission statement and goals are presented and parishioners are invited to complete their cards, which are collected right there.

Invitations

The council reviews the cards to determine whether all the goals will be covered and to look for key persons (in addition to organizations and existing committees) who need to be involved with each goal. Think about persons who have gifts or interests in a particular area, as well as any who might later block efforts. If they have not signed up, they should be called and *invited personally.* It is crucial that there be parish ownership and investment in the plan prior to this meeting. It is also helpful to have some sense of the degree of interest among parishioners—and to recruit others.

At the Assembly

Identify spaces in the hall where the break-out goal sessions will be held. Mark each one with a sign indicating the number and title of the goal. Pre-made name cards are possible at this assembly because of the sign-up; you may also want to color-code goals and name cards.

Planning the Second Assembly of the Start-up Process

An example of how one parish planned its second assembly

Publicity Group

Implemented a plan for getting interest stirred up in the parish

- Draft of mission statement and the goals published in the bulletin
- Homily addressing the draft of the mission statement and goals
- Display on bulletin boards
- Planned Goal Sign-up Sunday (see pp. 139-40 on Goal Sign-up Sunday)
- Phone follow-up to ensure ownership and involvement of key persons

Prayer and Process Group

Organized the assembly's content, schedule, procedures

- See First Assembly
- Planned prayer in format similar to that of First Assembly; reading was the mission statement, sharing question based on mission statement. End of prayer was the affirmation of parish goals (see sample, p. 157).
- Prepared text for formal ratification and affirmation for the pastor and/or other leaders.
- Determined which council members would sit with each goal group, who would facilitate and who would record

Hospitality Group

Made arrangements for physical details of assembly

- See First Assembly
- Arranged all data cards and compilations as part of prayer setting
- Set up room with large group seating and identified "goal areas" with blackboards or newsprint around the edge of room

THE SECOND ASSEMBLY

An example of one parish's second assembly

6:00–7:00	See First Assembly
	Pastor gave warm welcome, invoked the Spirit in prayer, introduced the leader.
7:10	Leader continued the prayer with reading of mission statement and posed question around a sentence or phrase in the mission statement for faith sharing.
7:20	Leader invited council members to explain how they wrote document, their difficulties throughout the process.
	Leader gave overview of the assembly, explaining how consensus is reached.
7:30	Leader led discussion on the mission statement toward consensus, taking one sentence at a time and allowing for comments—supportive or questioning.
	Leader sought a general sense of agreement with each sentence, while allowing "objectors" to state their case.
	Leader continued to test the group until there was general agreement, or at least until people could live with the decision of the whole.
	Pastor led ratification of the mission statement when consensus was reached.
	Leader conducted discussion of goals toward consensus (same as above).
	Pastor led affirmation of the goals when consensus was reached.
	Leader explained the work of the second half (brainstorming for objectives) and told the people to go to their marked "goal areas" after break.
8:00	Break
8:15	Each small group facilitator explained brainstorming.
	Groups brainstormed and recorded all ideas on newsprint.
	When brainstorming slowed, facilitator asked participants to group ideas which were similar and to prioritize them.

8:45 Leader concluded by:

- summarizing the evening
- explaining the next step (council writing objectives using what the people had said)
- promising continuing communication
- offering thanks for attendance that evening
- extending invitation to join future implementation groups

8:55 Pastor added his thanks, hopes, and blessing to all.

Ongoing Renewal: The Annual Spring Assembly

Once the initial start-up period for pastoral planning is complete, pastoral councils enter the ongoing renewal process which updates the plan every year. There is no more essential part to the growth of the pastoral plan than consultation with the parish community.

After the evaluation of objectives has been completed, the agenda for an annual Spring Assembly can be finalized. The council will need to develop a format for convening the parish again. At this assembly, council members once again engage with parishioners in reviewing the seven essential elements of pastoral life and their vitality in the parish. A report on the past year's progress toward the goals and objectives is part of this meeting. Congratulations and thanks could be offered to those responsible for implementing the objectives. Updated information on changing parish statistics and trends as well as regional, ecumenical, and collaborative efforts may be presented. Finally, the three-to-five-year goal areas are put before the assembly for additional brainstorming. Where should we go next on this pastoral issue? With the input they have received, parishioners should be able to add additional suggestions for new objectives.

What is important is the communication process. Parishioners ought to know what's going on and how their ideas can fit into a parish plan. The annual assembly is a celebration of achievements, naturally, but it also provides for dreaming exciting possibilities for the parish. In whatever form it takes, the annual assembly gathers "the baptized" to seek their wisdom and contributions toward fulfilling the parish mission.

The annual assembly does not need to be as formal as the "start-up" assemblies, but it does need a good plan. The assembly could take many forms:

- a special gathering called to review the past, celebrate the present, and envision the future
- part of a lunch or brunch following the last Sunday liturgy
- the first or final event of a parish anniversary, feast day, or other celebration
- part of an evening prayer which incorporates reflection on the assembly agenda
- a gathering between two Sunday liturgies, if there is enough time
- the culmination of a parish mission, novena, renewal or retreat
- focus groups or neighborhood gatherings

After the assembly, the council returns to its task of shaping objectives—based on the input of the parishioners—for the next year. Once again, the entire parish is asked to ratify the mission statement, goals and objectives—the Parish Plan—and to help form new implementation teams based on the new objectives. Spring is the perfect season to plant new seeds in a parish life cycle.

CONTINUING TO GENERATE THE PARISH PASTORAL PLAN

Once a plan has been formulated, the process continues. The effort required for the start-up period is greater than the effort required subsequently, when the plan should simply evolve as a normal part of parish life. The council builds into its calendar and the parish calendar the expectation of an annual review and advancement of the plan to its next phase. The chart on this page illustrates the "back and forth" movement of pastoral planning for an ordinary year.

PARISH PASTORAL COUNCIL	PARISH AT LARGE
Offers implementers resources, support, and **oversight**	**Implements** objectives of pastoral plan
With implementers, **evaluates** progress/success with objectives	Implementers, with council, **evaluate** progress/success with objectives

PARISH PASTORAL COUNCIL

Plans Annual Spring Assembly for parish:

- progress reports
- celebration of parish life
- thanks to implementers
- generation of new objectives for upcoming year

PARISH AT LARGE

Participates in Annual Spring Assembly

- congratulates implementers
- contributes suggestions for new objectives
- signs up as potential implementers of new plan

PARISH PASTORAL COUNCIL

Prepares Parish Pastoral Plan

- gathers assembly data
- organizes, edits ideas into objectives
- determines implementation plan
- presents completed pastoral plan to parish and diocese

PASTORAL PLANNING IN ACTION: THE EXAMPLE OF ONE PARISH

PASTORAL COUNCIL PLANNING AT THE CHURCH OF THE WINEMAKER

The council had three preparatory meetings to develop and carry out the communication plan and to plan the First Assembly. They did all the organizational work needed and recruited people to carry out details, making special attempts to invite personally as many people as possible.

After the First Assembly, some council members organized all the responses. They then spent two long meetings hammering out the draft mission statement. They surfaced broad areas that needed attention and drafted the goals.

At a third meeting, they made plans for Goal Sign-up Sunday and organized the details for the Second Assembly. Again, they contacted personally any parishioner or staff member who might have special interest or expertise in any of the goal areas.

After the Second Assembly (when parishioners first ratified the mission statement and goals and then worked in interest groups to brainstorm possible objectives) the Council took all the information and determined which objectives could reasonably be completed in one year's time. They also determined who would be responsible for each of the objectives.

When all the pieces were in place, the council provided parishioners with a complete parish plan—mission statement, goals, and objectives. A copy of the plan was sent to the Diocese.

DATA GATHERED BY THE PASTORAL COUNCIL OF THE CHURCH OF THE WINEMAKER

Begun by Slovak miners in 1900. Three miles from St. Anthony's parish of Italian origins.

Population:

1209 parishioners, 437 families. Many people over 65. Last formal census (1982) indicated 163 widowed persons. Current estimates—over 200.

Latest sacramental statistics:

13 baptisms, 5 marriages, and 29 funerals.

Parish facilities:

Church, renovated 1978, made handicapped accessible 1989; large rectory in good repair; school building needing substantial repairs. (School closed in 1963; first floor maintained for CCD classes. Roof, plumbing, and heating system are weak.) Parish hall under church, used for most parish activities. New restrooms desirable.

Church attendance statistics:

Church seats 384. Mass attendance: 35 percent, about 420 people per weekend. 3 Masses—180 at 6:30 Saturday evening, 50 at 8:00 Sunday, 180-200 at 10:30 Sunday Mass.

Youth statistics:

17 children in neighboring Catholic elementary school and 6 teens in regional Catholic high school. 88 children in elementary catechetical programs. 14 teens attend youth ministry, including instructional, social, and service activities. Estimated: 70 to 100 children and 45 teens not involved in any parish religious formation efforts.

Active ministries in the parish:

Sodality, Christian Mothers, Rosary Altar (same 17–35 women involved)
Lectors, choir (no eucharistic ministers, cantors, greeters, or Liturgy of the Word with Children)
RCIA (4 people in last 7 years)
CCD teachers (5 women, 1 man—most have taught CCD for at least ten years)

Most important parish activities:

Picnic, Mardi Gras, Mother's Day Breakfast, St. Patrick's Day Dance, Christmas Dinner, Blood Drive, Mom's House Party, Giving Tree

Most important parish fundraisers:

Tickets, Bingo, special collections for particular projects, car raffle at the parish picnic

Employment patterns:

Changed dramatically over the past twenty years, with the closure of both a nearby mine and a local tool and die plant. These two had provided for 65 percent of the jobs in town. Many younger families have moved, or wage earners travel up to 60 miles away for work. No draw for young people to stay in the area.

In town:

Lutheran and Methodist churches; just outside town, two relatively new free Bible churches.

Friendly relations among pastor and two ministers in town, but little done by way of actual collaboration. County office for human services in town, but people are proud and "take care of their own" even though services for food, health care, and counseling are available.

People from Church of the Winemaker support food pantry and small St. Vincent de Paul store sponsored by St. Anthony's. A few elderly parishioners go to the Lutheran senior center program for hot lunches and activities.

QUESTIONS USED AT THE FIRST ASSEMBLY

These questions were prepared on colored index cards, one question on each card. After people wrote down their answers and discussed them, they were collected and collated, then placed on the altar during the period of developing the pastoral plan.

1. If Jesus were here today, what words would he give to us to direct our future?

2. Why do you think the universal Catholic Church exists?

3. What is the makeup of this parish?

4. What do I as a member expect of my parish?

5. How should we reach out to the broader community from our parish?

6. What do our demographics and data suggest that we do for the future?

7. Which of the seven essential elements do we need to focus on and why?

PARISHIONERS' RESPONSES TO QUESTIONS

1. **If Jesus were here today, what words would he give us to direct our future?**
   - love one another, help each other
   - continue to work with your church family and to worship
   - live good Christian lives, giving example of love and good will to the young
   - spread the faith, keep it alive and growing
   - be true to My teachings
   - build on the faith we share and work together for the common good
   - live in love and fellowship, working to build a kingdom of peace
   - use the wisdom of the elders to guide the youngsters
   - continue to have faith and pray
   - stand up for your rights, but never hurt others as you do it
   - teach our children about cooperation and open-mindedness
   - forgive, be patient
   - help our children and families to preserve the ways of family life
   - honor and respect our older people
   - don't be judgmental
   - live in peace with one another
   - help and visit the sick

2. **Why does the universal Catholic Church exist?**
   - to celebrate Eucharist
   - to enrich and fulfill its members with the promise of eternal life
   - to keep the Body of Christ alive through faith
   - to pass on the apostolic tradition from Peter
   - to keep the life of Christ alive through the scriptures
   - to preserve the truth given us through the scriptures
   - to preserve the unity of all Catholic churches in the world
   - to give us the example of all the saints
   - because Christ founded the Church and built it on the rock of Peter
   - to keep the love of Christ alive
   - to maintain the doctrines of the Church found in the Creed
   - to provide the great leadership of our Pope and pass on the faith we have
   - to administer the sacraments
   - to preserve traditions

3. **What is the makeup of this parish community?**
   - conservative, economically depressed, not many job opportunities
   - multigenerational families, even though young families are moving to the city
   - rural parish, composed of working people
   - good, hard-working people
   - mostly elderly citizens, descendants of miners, steel workers, and factory workers
   - many on public assistance
   - unstable economy
   - old community, high on traditions
   - proud and caring people who look out for each other
   - scenic countryside, beautiful and quiet
   - 70 percent retired
   - friendly, cooperative people—not "shirkers"
   - church is very important

4. **What do I as a member expect of my parish?**
   - good leadership from the pastor
   - sense of ownership and concern from parishioners
   - community and community activities
   - devotional programs like novenas and benediction
   - that it will be here for my children
   - more work on evangelization, especially for the fallen-away Catholics
   - encourage more attendance at parish activities and CCD
   - stronger CCD program for our children, some adult education
   - more for families
   - cooperation between the young and the aged
   - visiting and helping the sick
   - missions to involve all ages in the church
   - well-attended Masses
   - more involvement of the teens and youth
   - get "new faces" involved instead of the same people all the time
   - reach out and help those who have less
   - everyone would be involved in at least one activity, be a worker, not a fault finder
   - area of evangelization needs to be addressed
   - better communication
   - more spiritual activities for families

5. **How should we reach out to the broader community?**
   - friendship and open arms
   - reach out to them in charity
   - with welcome and acceptance; cooperation in community events
   - provide opportunities for social activities in the community
   - open our functions to everyone in the area

- go out and help the needy
- fellowship
- greater development of community projects to alleviate our common problems
- our actions and words should really show our faith in God
- courtesy and cooperation

6. **What do our demographics and data suggest that we do for the future?**
   - deal with unemployment and families suffering because of it
   - review the Mass schedule, especially early Sunday
   - recruit more children and teens for religious education
   - try to get more parishioners active in parish activities and groups
   - do planning for elderly outreach with other churches in town
   - begin dialogue with nearby Catholic parish to do some things together (teens, elderly, RCIA, etc.)
   - let people know about available social services
   - add more liturgical ministries
   - work on evangelization
   - renew religious education program
   - do a complete census
   - review need for old school building

7. **Which of the seven essential elements do we need to focus on and why?**
   - Evangelization, because we're losing members and gaining few new ones
   - Word, especially in religious education for all ages and for families
   - Service, because so many people around here are hurting, struggling financially
   - Worship, because it is one thing that involves everyone and we have quite a way to go

NOTE: A few parishioners said other things, but the majority of people stressed the above.

Goal Areas Selected and Defined

Goal areas selected by the council from the data collected

1. Evangelization

2. Religious Education

3. Care for the Elderly

Because there was concern that people didn't know what was going on in the parish, the first phase of evangelization was to publicize and welcome people to parish programs and events.

Because the parish was very family-oriented, they determined that they wanted a family-focused religious education program.

There was recognition that the elderly needed personal contact from parishioners, so this goal was shaped with visiting at its heart.

Goals were defined as follows:

Goal I—*To increase evangelization efforts through communication*

Goal II—*To involve families in the religious education of their children*

Goal III—*To establish a parish visitation program*

Brainstorming on Objectives

Some ideas submitted from the goal group sessions at Second Assembly:

To increase evangelization efforts through communication
- have a bulletin insert
- distribute flyers at CCD classes
- deliver a brochure about the church to every house in the parish
- buy a billboard ad twice a year with messages about our church
- do a parish newsletter
- list all parish groups and activities in one booklet
- put the names of leaders of organizations and their phone numbers in the bulletin
- give information to the telephone "news line" to pass on the word

To involve families in the religious education of their children
- teach the Catechism
- start a new youth ministry
- have a mission
- organize a folk choir for the younger people
- get new books for our children
- get parents involved in CCD
- use married couples for baptismal preparation
- help parents of teens learn how to cope with today's problems

To establish a parish visitation program
- volunteer to help out at the Lutheran senior center because our people go there
- get the Girl Scouts to do things for the nursing home
- keep a telephone tree active to let people know who's in the hospital
- be sure Father visits every sick person on First Friday
- send get well cards to the sick and grieving
- do something for our widows

Some of these ideas seemed more feasible than others and were formed into concrete objectives by the council.

Church of the Winemaker Pastoral Plan

MISSION STATEMENT

We, the Church of the Winemaker, are an old, rural community of hardworking descendants of miners, steel and factory workers. Various ethnic orientations, proud traditions, and a strong sense of family unity enrich our parish life.

We are a Catholic community committed to keeping our faith alive and growing. We nurture this faith by celebrating the Eucharist, living out the scriptures, being true to church teachings and receiving the sacraments.

We hope to reflect the life and love of Jesus by strengthening the faith of our families and by reaching out to our neighbors.

Ratified at a Parish Assembly, __/__/__

GOALS AND OBJECTIVES

GOAL I:
To increase evangelization efforts through communication
(*RELATED TO ELEMENT OF EVANGELIZATION*)

1. To create a neighborhood telephone network for the purpose of sharing parish news by 08/__.
2. To establish a newsletter that will highlight current activities of the parish by 09/__.
3. to create a brochure to be renewed yearly that explains ongoing ministries and activities and lists names of parish personnel and parish leaders by 01/__.
4. To produce a monthly calendar as a bulletin insert every first Sunday of the month beginning 12/__.

GOAL II:
To involve families in the religious education of their children
(*RELATED TO ELEMENT OF WORD*)

1. To train two married couples with children in baptism preparation by 12/__.
2. To provide one parent-to-parent baptism preparation session in 01/__ and one in 06/__.
3. To evaluate the total religious education program of the parish in consultation with the Office of Religious Formation by 06/__.
4. To plan a seminar entitled "Keeping Your Kids Catholic" (to be offered next year) for parents of junior and senior high school students by 03/__.

5. To offer a family day of reflection in 12/__ and in 03/ __ in consultation with the Office of Youth Ministry.

GOAL III:
To establish a parish visitation program
(RELATED TO ELEMENT OF SERVICE)

1. To institute a parish visitation program to our three local nursing homes by 12/__.
2. To plan and organize a peer visitation program for the widowed in the parish by 03/__.
3. To select and train Eucharistic Ministers to the homebound by 12/__.

Ratification of Mission Statement

Pastor: Before God and under the guidance of the Holy Spirit, we have prayed, discussed and shaped the mission of the Church of the Winemaker to reflect what we believe. Therefore, I ask your assent and commitment to the newly-affirmed Mission Statement of our parish. Please say AMEN in response to the following statements.

We, the Church of the Winemaker, are an old rural community of hardworking descendants of miners, steel and factory workers.

Parishioners: AMEN.

Pastor: Various ethnic orientations, proud traditions, and a strong sense of family unity enrich our parish life.

Parishioners: AMEN.

Pastor: We are a Catholic community, committed to keeping our faith alive and growing.

Parishioners: AMEN.

Pastor: We nurture this faith by celebrating the Eucharist, living out the scriptures, being true to church teachings, and receiving the sacraments.

Parishioners: AMEN.

Pastor: We hope to reflect the life and love of Jesus by strengthening the faith of our families and by reaching out to our neighbors.

Parishioners: AMEN.

Pastor: I now declare that this, indeed, is the mission of our parish community, the Church of the Winemaker.

Affirmation of Parish Goals

Pastor: Committed to our mission, we now affirm three goals which will direct us in fulfilling our mission during the next five years. Please respond WE DO to each of the following questions.

Do you believe that we are called, through better communication, to increase evangelization efforts in our parish?

Parishioners: WE DO.

Pastor: Do you believe that we are called to involve families in the religious education of their children?

Parishioners: WE DO.

Pastor: Do you believe that we are called to establish a parish visitation program?

Parishioners: WE DO.

Pastor: Therefore, I do hereby affirm that for the next five years we will strive to be directed by these goals and will assume responsibility for supporting them.

IV: THE MINISTRY OF LEADERSHIP

JESUS AS LEADER

- *Had a sense of vision or mission*
- *Empowered others for the mission*
- *Affirmed the gifts of others*
- *Gathered people together*
- *Collaborated with and empowered his disciples*
- *Reconciled the hurt and alienated*
- *Listened with empathy*
- *Served others*
- *Took risks*

PASTORAL COUNCIL LEADERSHIP

THE MINISTRY OF PASTORAL LEADERSHIP

Parishioners who serve on a parish pastoral council must be those who have received a call to the ministry of leadership. Together with the pastor, these are individuals who are capable of reflection, discernment, visioning, reaching consensus, and pastoral planning.

The following is a list of the gifts necessary for pastoral leadership:

- a desire for spiritual growth in oneself and the parish
- enthusiasm about the future of the parish
- eagerness to facilitate parish decisions about its direction
- courage to work toward consensus
- capacity to listen outweighing the need to speak
- integrity in articulating what one has heard and what one believes
- the ability to inspire and empower
- a willingness to delegate
- flexibility and openness with people and ideas

Pastoral council members ought to be individuals of faith who are capable of leading the parish in the discernment, expression, and fulfillment of its mission. Ideally, they are people of vision, open to the workings of the Holy Spirit in and through themselves, while having a deep respect and openness for the workings of the Spirit in others.

The clergy and parish staff, too, must possess and demonstrate this same disposition toward the ministry of shared leadership if the process is to be effective.

While the pastor and members of the council may possess the above qualities in varying degrees, it is important to nurture and strengthen these attributes over time. For this reason, the pastor and the council members ought to engage in initial and ongoing formation in the ministry of leadership, the essential elements of parish life, and the role of pastoral councils. This continuing education is critical to the effectiveness of the body. It is a way of ensuring the perpetual pouring of new wine into fresh wineskins.

It is also important that members of the parish leadership body have opportunities to pray with one another and to deepen their individual and communal holiness. To this end, the council should set aside at least fifteen minutes of each session for prayer. It is crucial for the clergy and council to model the seven essential elements themselves. In this way, the clergy and council form a microcosm of the parish community of faith.

The council may also join together for an annual retreat and/or periodic days of reflection as a means of strengthening the bonds of faith which bind them together and, in turn, to the parish and the total Church.

As transitions occur with changes in council membership and parish personnel or clergy assignments, all those who are new to the process should receive some formal orientation to the parish mission, the pastoral planning process, goals and objectives, and the model of shared leadership. This will ensure a continuity of shared vision.

The parish pastoral plan, then, becomes the consistent source of stability and direction in times of transition. New pastors receive from the bishop the pastoral plan as part of the official transfer process. Parish staff members affirm the parish plan as part of their commitment to the parish. So, too, do parishioners through their respect and support for the ongoing development of the mission, goals, and objectives of the parish. Thus shared leadership within the parish revolves around the pastoral plan as the focal point of everyone's labor in the vineyard.

Exploring the Leadership Task

People must think of us as Christ's servants, stewards entrusted with the mysteries of God. What is expected of stewards is that each one should be found worthy of this trust (1 Cor 4:1-2).

Jesus urges his disciples to resist the urge to lord it over people with an air of superiority even as he modeled an alternative: "The greatest among you must be your servant" (Matt 23: 11).

In the New Testament, a steward is an authoritative servant. The steward oversees the domestic order of the household, the rhythms, rules, and agreements which enable the household or community to thrive. In the New Testament and elsewhere, stewardship describes a leadership position reserved for experienced, capable persons.

Pastoral council members are to be leader/stewards. Organizing a committee to perform a task is only one small aspect of what is involved. Here is a checklist that describes the gifts and attitudes needed for this leadership ministry.

____ I do not do the parish's work; rather, I support the parish's life in the Spirit.

____ I foster the network of effective relationships throughout the parish.

____ I motivate others to act through direct personal contact with large numbers of people in the parish.

____ I motivate the parish in the pursuit of shared goals toward a common vision.

____ I contribute to bringing the council to life by participating in consensus decision making.

____ I nurture commitment to the group, by recognizing that "we are in this together."

____ I know how to lead others beyond their personal interests.

____ I see others as valued partners, not competitors.

____ I am not afraid of conflict, recognizing that diversity produces creativity.

____ I invite people to recognize their own gifts and offer these to the common vision.

____ I can recruit people to construct the future together.

____ I can move beyond coordinating plans already in place to activating new plans for the future.

____ I encourage openness to change.

____ I consistently express confidence in the parish's ability to succeed in making progress toward the goals.

____ I demonstrate empathy, understanding, encouragement, and support.

____ I am grateful to God daily for my gift of leadership.

Metaphors for Pastoral Leadership

Each of the following metaphors describes a type of leadership. Review them and write down what comes to your mind as you think of the kind of leadership each of them connotes. What qualities does each bring to the task of leadership? If you can think of others, add them to the list.

Army General

Boss

CEO

Coach

Cruise Ship Social Coordinator

Daddy

Dictator

Financial Administrator

Negotiator

Orchestra Conductor

Plant Manager

Public Relations Director

Servant

Spiritual Director

Teacher

Other

Shared Leadership

First think about your response to the following, and then discuss your responses with other council members:

1. Name five qualities individually needed by members of a leadership team such as the pastoral council:

2. Name three activities you believe are essential to the healthy maintenance of leadership teams:

3. What are your feelings about shared leadership?

4. What attitudes, behavior preferences, or beliefs can be obstacles to shared leadership?

5. What can you do to facilitate shared leadership as a pastoral council member?

EMPOWERMENT

LEADERSHIP AND EMPOWERMENT

Perhaps the one task that is most essential in "getting things done" at a parish is that of empowering others. When the plan is complete, the council's work really begins. The council's responsibility lies not in carrying out the plan, but in seeing that parishioners are invited, encouraged, supported, and challenged to do so. As part of their stewardship, the baptized are called to participate in the parish by active involvement in its ongoing life. Council members convey that truth to the people and spend time finding the right match between the gifts of parishioners and the tasks that need to be done.

After the plan is completed, the council table becomes a brainstorming center as council members try to identify people who can implement the objectives. Parish organizations as well as individuals can be recruited. Using information gathered at assemblies and other parish-wide efforts to search out people's and talents, council members can make phone calls or talk to people after Mass to invite participation on implementation teams. Once formed, these teams receive encouragement and support from the council as the plan moves from paper into action.

Empowerment: What It Is and Isn't

EMPOWERMENT IS:

A way to involve people in decisions and actions

A leadership skill built on human dynamics

A shared goal and the support and direction needed to achieve it

Delegating both responsibility and accountability

EMPOWERMENT ISN'T:

Dumping a project on someone

An easy way to get something done

Micro-management of the details of a project

Giving someone freedom to act without accountability

What's Needed for Empowerment

Empowered people work together to accomplish common goals and objectives.

To maximize their potential and succeed in attaining objectives, individuals and groups responsible for implementation must have:

Data

Implementers need timely and accurate information regarding matters that impact their work. Leaders need to keep communication frequent and substantive. Both positive and negative data needs to be shared openly.

Authority

Implementers are authorized to follow through on the objective for which they are responsible, but they are not simply abandoned to fend for themselves. They are expected to develop an action plan, discuss their needs with the council, and then proceed with implementation. An evaluation is expected upon completion of the task, as well as interim reports if the task is extensive.

Resources

While the implementers themselves are a parish's greatest resource, most objectives will require additional resources. The council needs to ensure that those responsible for a task have these resources, whether material, fiscal, or personnel. If the undertaking is significant, the council should budget for it prior to start-up.

Skills

Selecting and empowering individuals or groups is not a random process. The council needs to assess the skills needed for a particular task and seek out those with the gifts to carry it out effectively. If some additional training is desirable, leaders see to it that skill development is available.

Active Support

Empowerment of implementation teams requires that the council provide:

Clarity—Giving a clear picture of the task to be accomplished and the end result expected; sharing how it is related to the parish mission

Commitment—Demonstrating enthusiasm for the project and getting the energetic support and involvement of the implementers

Encouragement—Keeping in touch with the implementers as activity progresses, not to supervise the project but to offer encouragement and support

Gratitude—Showing appreciation for the efforts expended and the results of the activity, especially for the service rendered to the parish and its mission

DIS-EMPOWERING FACTORS

- Confusion with regard to the nature and scope of the project
- Lack of trust between implementers and council
- Failures in communication and listening
- Politics, factions, conditions perceived as needless "red tape"
- Projects that are too tightly structured, with all problems solved by council ahead of time
- Insufficient resources, lack of skills
- Belief that the task is meaningless or won't make a difference

Strategies for Effective Empowerment

"It's the same people doing the same thing around here!"

Sound familiar? The time has come to turn this all-too-often-expressed complaint around. Sometimes the problem is certainly apathy on the part of parishioners, but often the problem is actually the way in which leaders present projects and requests.

A parish pastoral plan starting with a broad mission statement, broad goals, and clear, defined objectives is the key. The more specific the request, the more likely it is that a smart person or group will say yes—even more so if the request is made with enthusiasm and passion for the vision of the parish.

Here are several strategies and attitudes that should help:

1. Be sure objectives are specific and time-bound. Respect for the time, energy, and family lives of the parishioners will be appreciated. They are more likely to volunteer if they are sure of what they are being asked to do and can see an end to the activity. Example: "Sarah, would you be willing to join four other people in being trained this year to lead the Liturgy of the Word with Children? There will be three training sessions that will take place on . . ." instead of, "Sarah, would you be in charge of beginning Liturgy of the Word with Children in our parish?"

2. Take care to match the objective with the gift and interest of the person or group. Believe that your parish has all the gifts needed for your unique mission. Those who have a natural inclination to the task will be more successful and experience less stress.

3. Motivate with your own enthusiasm. Positive, upbeat attitudes are catchy. Others want to be part of something that is energizing and purposeful. Requests with a negative, pessimistic, or sarcastic attitude don't work.

4. Strategize with the personal touch. Here are some suggestions. Use phone calls. Invite individuals and organizations personally to attend assemblies or to become part of the parish vision by implementing a particular objective. Prepare creative, catchy mailings. Plan to maximize the after-Mass encounters.

5. Give feedback along the way. When monitoring the objectives during the year, always remember to thank volunteers for their time and talent.

6. Conduct a formal evaluation of each objective as closure to the project. People are more likely to volunteer again when they feel as if they have accomplished something for the good of the whole and they have been asked for their assessment of the project.

A Checklist of Empowerment Skills for Parish Pastoral Council Leaders

- ☐ Do I motivate with my enthusiasm?
- ☐ Do I use a personal touch when I recruit, matching gifts and talents with the request?
- ☐ Do I provide a promise of training (if necessary) with the request for service?
- ☐ Do I continue to nurture and affirm individuals and groups throughout the year?
- ☐ Do I take time to evaluate with the individual or group, pointing out successes and learning from failures?
- ☐ Am I able to "let go" after I provide the individual or group with proper information and resources, so they are free to creatively accomplish the objective?
- ☐ Do I affirm outstanding performance appropriately?

Empowerment in Action: One Example

This example demonstrates how one aspect of a pastoral plan was conceived and brought to fruition in a parish.

➤ Assembly to gather ideas of parishioners . . .

Lots of parishioners attend assembly to contribute ideas they've been thinking about.

Council collates all ideas submitted, finds many grouped around one big idea, Religious Education of Parish Children. Others concerned about adult faith development.

➤ Council decides that the pastoral plan must reflect this idea, so they draft a goal which reads:

To implement a total religious formation program for the parish.

➤ At second parish assembly, parishioners unanimously ratify the goal. They brainstorm on bringing goal to life. Many indicate willingness to work on potential activities.

➤ Council takes more than thirty-five ideas suggested, consults with parish coordinator of religious education, and determines three major steps they can accomplish in coming year. These are objectives:

1. To select several appropriate models of religious education for children by __/__/__.

2. To institute four seasonal family-based evenings of religious formation by __/__/__.

3. To establish a parish lending library of books, magazines and audiovisual materials for religious education by __/__/__.

➤ Objective #1 appeals to several young parents. Coordinator of religious education brings them together with three experienced teachers in existing parish CCD program. This implementation group of twelve persons develops a task list, a timeline, and a budget for the year:

- Some will meet with the Diocesan Catechetical Office in August.
- Some will attend a workshop on specialized programs in September.
- Some will visit three other parishes which are using different materials in October.
- Some will interview parents in small groups about their expectations between October and December.
- Some will examine sample copies of materials at the diocesan office and order sample copies of things which might be useful to them by November.

- Total implementation group meets again in January. Members share information and select seven different programs. Decide to sponsor information evening for parents in order to present findings and get feedback.

- At information evening, member of implementation group explains each program. Parents talk in small groups, ask questions, examine materials. Before leaving, each family selects three programs which best match their expectations for children's religious education.

- Results are tallied. Five highest ranked programs are researched for training and materials costs. Interim report is prepared for council.

- Council takes the budgetary figures to meeting with finance council.

- After councils meet, $5000 is allocated for the implementation of this objective in the following year. Pastoral council informs implementation group of this, advising them to select the resources they deem best.

- One option is eliminated because of time involved in training, another because of its excessive cost. Three programs are adopted as options for religious formation of children in the coming year.

- Evaluation revealed:
    - Implementation group worked very well together; coordinator of religious education feeling very confident about progress being made.
    - Two of the programs chosen as options stressed family involvement and home-based activities.
    - Parents were genuinely interested, but worried about their ability to participate in religious formation of their children.

- Spring Assembly applauded the process and final results. Implementation group indicated energy to re-invest in next phase of project. New interest from at least a dozen parents.

- The process gave rise to new objectives for following year:

    1. *To implement and evaluate three new models of religious formation*

    2. *To offer a six-week course in the fall on religion and parenting skills*

    3. *To train neighborhood catechetical coordinators in one of the new programs*

PARISH ROLES AND REPONSIBILITIES

FULFILLING THE PARISH MISSION THROUGH LEADERSHIP ROLES AND RELATIONSHIPS

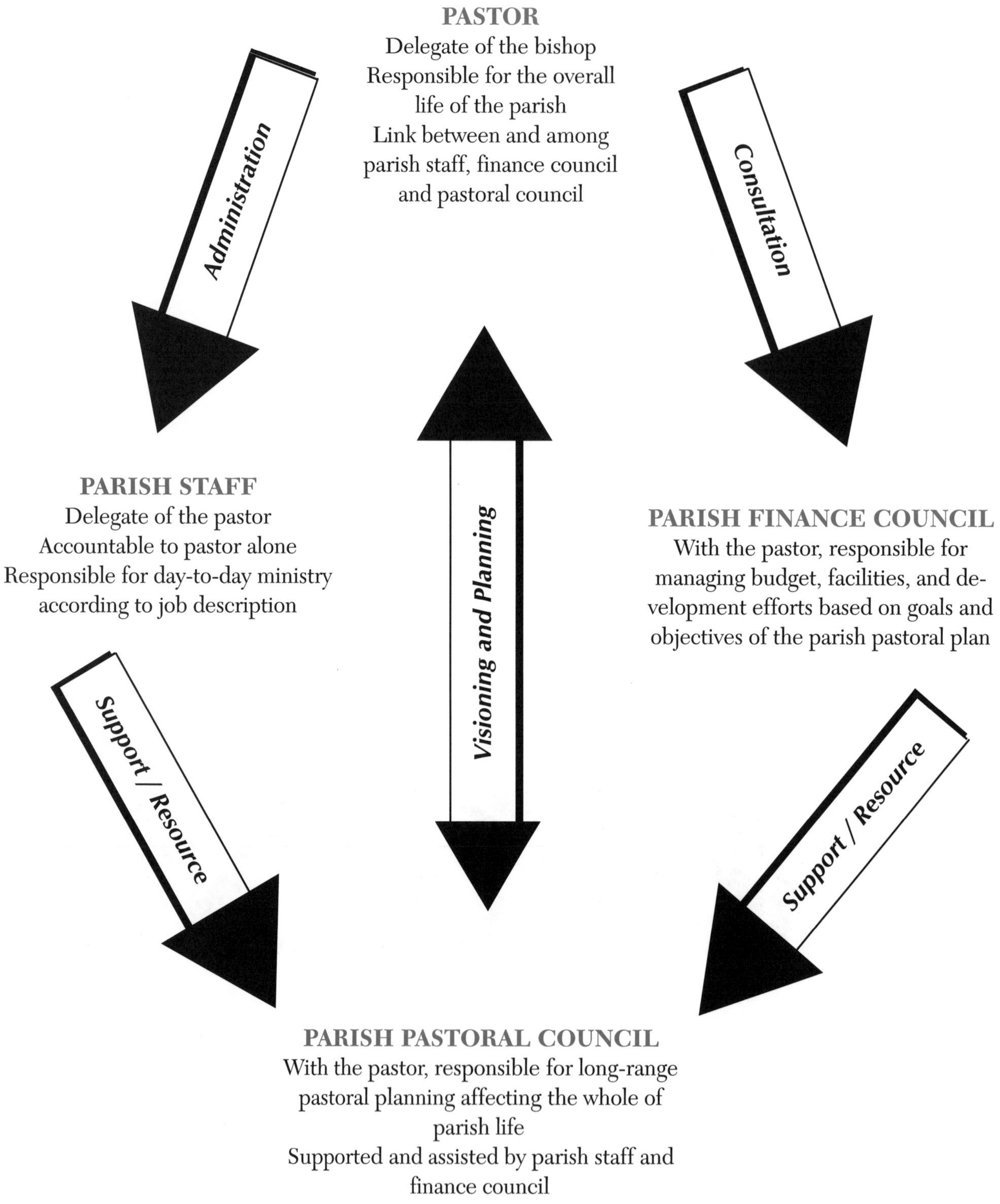
PASTOR
Delegate of the bishop
Responsible for the overall life of the parish
Link between and among parish staff, finance council and pastoral council
Administration
Consultation
Visioning and Planning
PARISH STAFF
Delegate of the pastor
Accountable to pastor alone
Responsible for day-to-day ministry according to job description
PARISH FINANCE COUNCIL
With the pastor, responsible for managing budget, facilities, and development efforts based on goals and objectives of the parish pastoral plan
Support / Resource
Support / Resource
PARISH PASTORAL COUNCIL
With the pastor, responsible for long-range pastoral planning affecting the whole of parish life
Supported and assisted by parish staff and finance council

Role of Pastor

Historically and canonically, the pastor is the individual who bears ultimate responsibility for the parish. From the earliest days of the Church, leaders arose from within the Christian community who instructed the faithful, oversaw the ministries of the community, and endeavored to keep the assembly faithful to the Gospel of Jesus Christ:

> Some people God has designated in the church to be, first, apostles; second, prophets; third teachers; then, mighty deeds; then, gifts of healing, assistance, administration, and varieties of tongues. (1 Cor 12:28)

> And he gave some as apostles, others as prophets, others as evangelists, others as pastors and teachers, to equip the holy ones for the work of ministry, for building up the body of Christ. . . . (Eph 4:11-12)

Clearly, there were pastors called forth to lead the earliest Christian communities. The particular gifts of these individuals for the ministry of leadership were to be placed at the service of all. Together, pastors and members of the community were to work as one in the service of the Gospel:

> There are different kinds of spiritual gifts but the same Spirit; there are different forms of service but the same Lord; there are different workings but the same God who produces all of them in everyone. (1 Cor 12:4-6)

While it is evident that the role and leadership responsibilities associated with a pastor and ordained ministers have always been present within the Christian community, the ministry of the pastor/priest has evolved and been further defined through the centuries.

The documents of Vatican II shed distinct light on the role of the ordained clergy and of pastors in particular. In the Decree on the Ministry and Life of Priests (*Presbyterorum Ordinis*) we read:

> Through the sacred ordination and mission which they receive from the bishops, priests are promoted to the service of Christ the Teacher, Priest and King; they are given a share in his ministry, through which the Church here on earth is being ceaselessly built up into the People of God, Christ's Body, and the temple of the Spirit. . . .

> The Lord also appointed certain men as ministers. . . . These men were to hold in the community of the faithful the sacred power of Order, that of offering sacrifice and forgiving sins, and were to exercise the priestly office publicly on behalf of [all] in the name of Christ.

"Together, pastors and members of the community were to work as one in the service of the Gospel."

The priests of the New Testament are, it is true, by their vocation to ordination, set apart in some way in the midst of the People of God, but this is not in order that they should be separated from that people . . . but that they should be completely consecrated to the task for which God chooses them.

> Finally, priests have been placed in the midst of the laity so that they may lead them all to the unity of charity. . . . Theirs is the task, then, of bringing about agreement among divergent outlooks in such a way that nobody may feel a stranger in the Christian community.[26]

The Council also indicated that pastors bear a particular responsibility to enable the development of the Christian community which has been entrusted to their care and leadership:

> The pastors, indeed, should recognize and promote the dignity and responsibility of the laity in the Church. They should willingly use their prudent advice and confidently assign duties to them in the service of the Church, leaving them freedom and scope for acting. Indeed, they should give them the courage to undertake works on their own initiative.
>
> Many benefits for the Church are to be expected from this familiar relationship between the laity and the pastors. . . . Strengthened by all her members, the Church can thus more effectively fulfill her mission for the life of the world.[27]

The Code of Canon Law likewise has a substantial amount to say about the role and responsibilities of the pastor. For example, the following canons emphasize the central place of the pastor in the life of the parish community:

> The pastor is the proper shepherd of the parish entrusted to him, exercising pastoral care in the community entrusted to him under the authority of the diocesan bishop in whose ministry of Christ he has been called to share; in accord with the norm of law he carries out for his community the duties of teaching, sanctifying and governing, with the cooperation of other presbyters or deacons and the assistance of lay members of the Christian faithful. (Canon 519)

To assume the office of pastor validly, one must be in the sacred order of the presbyterate. He should also be distinguished for his sound doctrine and integrity of morals and endowed with a zeal for souls and other virtues. (Canon 521, §§1,2)

> In order to fulfill his office in earnest the pastor should strive to come to know the faithful who have been entrusted to his

> care. . . . The pastor is to acknowledge and promote the proper role which the lay members of the Christian faithful have in the Church's mission. . . . (Canon 529, 1, 2)

The pastor, then, has primary role of leadership in both the spiritual and temporal affairs of the parish. He is held accountable by the Church for the well-being of the parish. The laity are to assist him in whatever way possible, and he is to welcome and take into serious account their opinions and recommendations. Ultimately, all decisions about the operation and direction of the parish need to carry his agreement and approval. The pastor leads the community by example, empowerment of others, appropriate delegation of authority, and participation in the pastoral planning process. His ownership of the pastoral mission is essential if it is to come to fruition in the life of the parish community.

"The pastor is to . . . promote the proper role which lay members have in the Church's mission . . ."

Role of the Parish Staff

Parish staff members include such professionals as parochial vicars, pastoral associates, catechetical leaders, Catholic school principals, liturgists, or others who bear the responsibility, under specific job descriptions, for implementing major dimensions of parish life.

Their relationship to the pastoral council may vary. In some parishes, they may participate in council meetings as consultants or resource persons. Whether they regularly attend meetings or not, it is important that they be kept informed of the council's direction by the pastor.

Likewise, parish staff members may seek the support and advice of the council in areas for which they are responsible under their job descriptions. They share responsibility with the pastor for keeping the council abreast of new directions in church and diocesan programs, especially when these will have an impact on how the parish mission statement is carried out.

Roles within the Pastoral Council

The pastoral council serves as a consultative body to the pastor.[28] It needs to be made clear that the pastoral visioning and planning function of the council and the day-to-day administrative operations of the parish are two separate and distinct areas of responsibility. The pastor, parochial vicar(s), and parish staff are responsible for routine decision-making which needs to take place for the parish to function efficiently and effectively on a daily basis. Daily decision-making is the responsibility of those whose job description encompasses such judgments. These day-to-day operational decisions are not the responsibility of the pastoral council, whose role is to guide the community in the discernment, expression, and fulfillment of its pastoral mission.

Aside from the pastor, who serves as presider, council members serve in a variety of roles. These council roles may be performed by certain individuals for an indefinite period of time, lending continuity and stability to the process. Councils may want to rotate these roles on a periodic basis, but would be best served by not doing so too often.

THE PRESIDER (PASTOR)

The pastor leads the process of discernment, expression, and fulfillment of the parish's mission in his role as PRESIDER of the parish pastoral council. He attends all meetings of the council and participates in the discussion and decision-making process. Prior to the group's coming to consensus, the pastor is obligated to raise questions or objections relating to issues that could affect the outcome of the decision. When consensus occurs, the pastor ratifies the decision.

In his role as presider, the pastor does not facilitate the meetings but rather oversees and participates in all council deliberations. He sheds light on church teachings and parish or diocesan background and/or guidelines, and actively listens to council's deliberations. "Because he is ultimately responsible for the care of the parish, the pastor presides at the parish council in a way strikingly similar to his presidency at the Eucharist."[29] Here, too, he leads the community in its expression of the seven essential elements of the parish life.

Tasks:

- sets agenda with the facilitator and recorder
- sees that the council performs its duties
- sees to the ongoing development and training of council members
- gives the council direction and assistance when necessary
- is accountable for the quality of the decisions of the council

Techniques:

- empowers the council to leadership
- becomes an active participant in the consensus process
- gives the council feedback, support, and affirmation
- keeps an open mind

THE CONVENER

The CONVENER is the person responsible for reserving the meeting space, preparing whatever materials are needed for the meeting, and generally making sure that the environment is conducive for the meeting and that the necessary practical preparations have been made. The convener works with the recorder to ensure that members are adequately informed and reminded of the meeting date and time.

Tasks:

- provides the last call to remind everyone of the meeting
- prepares the essentials:
  - resources (books, documents, diocesan guidelines)
  - materials (charts, newsprint, markers, tape, videos)
  - equipment that works (VCR, tape player, projector)
- arranges the room:
  - well lighted, well ventilated room(a lack of oxygen drains mind and body!)
  - comfortable physical setup for a small group
- hospitality:
  - welcomes members to the meeting
  - provides light refreshments

Techniques:

- creates an atmosphere of hospitality and comfort for relaxed concentration
- chooses space that fits the group
- arranges table, chairs in a way that facilitates eye-to-eye contact
- makes friends with the janitor or maintenance crew
- keeps interruptions during the meeting to a minimum by getting rid of distractions (including unwanted noise)

THE FACILITATOR

A person capable of serving in the role of FACILITATOR is also to be selected from among the members. This individual designs and oversees the process of each council meeting, assisting the group with planning, decision-making, and problem solving. The facilitator is not a chairperson to whom comments are addressed, but rather someone who assists the group in fulfilling its tasks and responsibilities.

Tasks:

- prepares the agenda with the presider and recorder
- is the servant of the group, not its authority leader
- focuses the group on a common task
- encourages everyone to participate
- is neutral, not evaluating the ideas of others
- contributes his/her ideas only after stepping aside from role
- suggests alternatives, varies methods and procedures
- helps arrive at win/win solutions

Techniques:

- defines issues clearly
- does not have all the answers, but refers questions back to council members
- maintains a positive atmosphere, giving positive feedback and compliments
- doesn't talk too much
- isn't afraid to make mistakes or to seek clarifications
- isn't defensive
- asks the council for a critique of his/her role

THE RECORDER

The RECORDER keeps track of the progress of each meeting and records official decisions for reference. The recorder is also responsible for any council correspondence or other clerical tasks, including disseminating the agenda and meeting reminders to the council in advance of each meeting. The recorder may also be the designated contact with the media and/or diocesan or local newspapers for publicity on newsworthy items.

Tasks:

- prepares agenda with presider and facilitator
- keeps a record of basic information, decisions, assignments of council—not a detailed set of "minutes"
- in important discussions, keeps a public record before the council, recording on an overhead transparency or a newsprint tablet
- remains neutral, and contributes his/her ideas only after stepping aside from role
- provides copies of the record within a week of the meeting
- disseminates pertinent information to council members between meetings

Techniques:

- listens for key words, basic ideas, the essence of the record
- writes legibly and quickly when doing public recording
- uses abbreviations, is unconcerned about spelling
- stops the group and asks for repetition if ideas are coming too fast
- isn't defensive if someone calls for a correction
- uses markers, variations in size of writing, symbols (stars, arrows, dots) to indicate importance and relationship of data
- numbers, titles, and dates all sheets

THE AGENDA TEAM

The AGENDA TEAM consists of the pastor, facilitator, and recorder. These three individuals meet ahead of time to formulate the meeting's agenda and discuss practical arrangements for the meeting. This information is then communicated to the convener, and the recorder sends the agenda and any other necessary materials to the council members.

Tasks and Techniques:

1. Formulates the agenda for each council meeting
   - reviews previous meetings' agendas for unfinished business
   - consults the annual planning cycle to identify current items: evaluating the parish plan, planning an assembly, meeting the finance council, scheduling a retreat, orienting new parish personnel
   - reviews council skill development needs: coming to consensus, understanding roles, empowering implementers, learning to pray

2. Considers practical matters related to council meeting
   - seeks a speaker or other resource
   - arranges for changes in time or place of meeting
   - researches any topics that will be discussed
   - decides about pre-meeting study materials

3. Assigns tasks for the meeting
   - communicates special prayer needs to spiritual formation team
   - engages transition team if there are transitional issues
   - invites any special guests, consultants, staff persons
   - alerts convener to any special needs for the meeting
   - prepares materials needed for meeting (with convener or recorder)
   - issues the agenda at least a week in advance to council members (with recorder)
   - calls council members to remind them about time, place, agenda at least three days in advance (with convener)

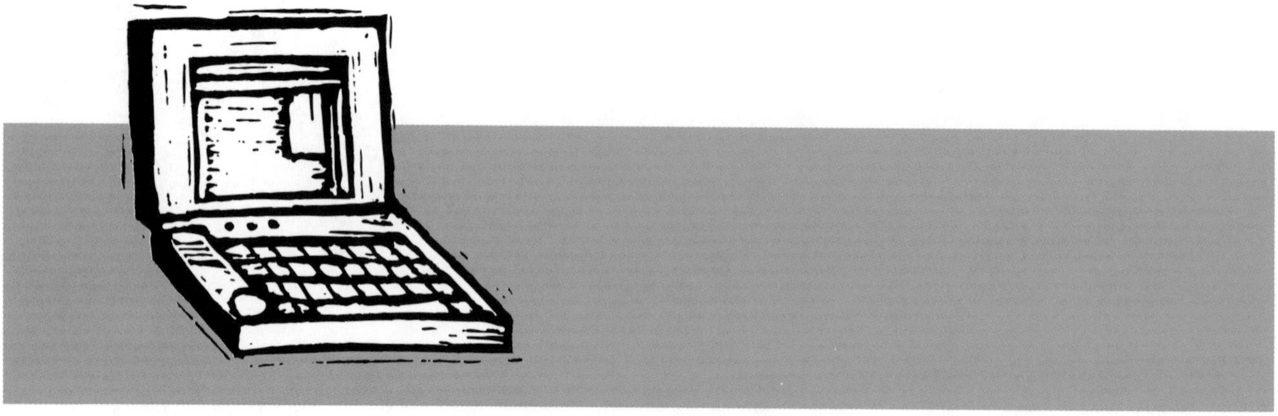

THE TRANSITION TEAM

The TRANSITION TEAM is responsible for the initial and ongoing training/education of members and for coordinating the selection of new members when transitions occur. This team is also responsible for orienting new parish staff members to the parish mission and to the goals and objectives of the pastoral plan. When transitions occur in the persons of the pastor and/or parochial vicar(s), the transition team provides an orientation to the mission for newly assigned clergy as well.

Tasks and Techniques:

1. Arranges for ongoing council education on REVISIONING THE PARISH PASTORAL COUNCIL
   - reviews the seven essential elements of parish life to determine annual areas of study and reflection
   - procures materials on the elements for the council resource shelf
   - seeks sources of input on topics chosen: skills of council, mission statement of parish, elements underlying parish goals
   - plans for council attendance at diocesan-sponsored ongoing education events and programs

2. Carries out the transition and orientation of new parish personnel
   - arranges for closure activities for outgoing personnel, such as pastor, parochial vicar, parish staff member, or council members. Could include: communication, liturgy, farewell celebration, acknowledgments. In the case of a new pastor, coordinates any official transitional activities with diocesan staff.
   - arranges parish welcoming activities, installation ceremonies, or other appropriate celebrations.
   - plans and carries out council orientation for new parish personnel. Could include: social, introductions to members, parish history, mission, goals, implementation, evaluation to date.

3. Coordinates the selection process for new council members (see detailed information in the section entitled "Selecting New Council Members," pp. 192-198).

THE SPIRITUAL FORMATION TEAM

The SPIRITUAL FORMATION TEAM plans programs of spiritual enrichment for council members. This team is also responsible for the preparation of the prayer/study segment of each meeting. It may also plan an annual retreat or periodic evenings of reflection for the council as important means of ongoing spiritual formation.

Tasks and Techniques:

1. Plans programs of spiritual enrichment
   - gets input from council to determine direction for spiritual growth
   - procures prayer/reflection materials for the council resource shelf
   - seeks sources of input on spiritual formation topics
   - plans for council attendance at diocesan-sponsored renewal programs

2. Prepares prayer/study portions of each meeting
   - considers the parish situation, liturgical season, council agenda, or other factors which would inform the prayer experience (with agenda team)
   - designs prayer with sensitivity to the need for song, silence, listening to God's word, sharing reflections, and general prayer for the council and parish needs
   - prepares all the details of the prayer— music, texts, rituals, and roles (with convener)

3. Designs evenings of prayer or an annual council retreat
   - reserves time for such during council calendar planning
   - develops ideas for themes and format
   - makes needed arrangements and prepares details

ALL COUNCIL MEMBERS

ALL COUNCIL MEMBERS have responsibility for the quality of council life and especially of its meetings. Even if all those with assigned roles—and many or most council members will serve in at least one role—perform their duties faithfully, without the preparation and participation of all members, the group will flounder. It behooves council members to spend some time in both remote and proximate preparation for the meetings.

Tasks and Techniques:

- prepare for every meeting by reviewing the agenda and the previous meeting's notes
- make a strong commitment to regular, on-time participation in council meetings
- complete "homework"—reading, duties for the meeting, assignments
- formulate what they honestly believe, but come willing to hear others
- sit in different places, avoid forming cliques
- enter into the prayer and faith sharing
- participate in the discussion, listen carefully to others
- avoid negative assumptions, defensiveness
- focus their energies on the issues at hand
- refuse to judge the motives of others, put words in their mouths, or cut them off in discussions
- keep the facilitator and recorder neutral
- assure that key ideas are accurately recorded
- give honest feedback and evaluation of the quality of the meeting

The council itself has no committee structure. It may, however, establish AD HOC IMPLEMENTATION GROUPS for the accomplishment of the yearly objectives established as part of the pastoral plan. These groups do not usually consist of council members but rather members of the parish at large. A council member may participate in the work of these groups if he or she has particular expertise related to the task, and the time and energy to do so.

Existing parish groups and/or committees may also be called upon to perform certain tasks or functions in light of the parish's pastoral plan. These persons, however, are not council members. Rather, all work together in different capacities and in consultation with one another toward the realization of the parish mission and the promotion of the Gospel.

Relationship to Parish Finance Council

The PARISH FINANCE COUNCIL serves as an advisory body to the pastor and the parish pastoral council in the administration and stewardship of parish finances, budget, parish facilities, and long-range financial development. Mandated by canon law, parish finance councils, like parish pastoral councils, are consultative bodies:

> Each parish is to have a finance council which is regulated by universal law as well as by norms issued by the diocesan bishop; in this council the Christian faithful, selected according to the same norms, aid the pastor in the administration of parish goods... (Canon 537)

Members of the finance council are appointed by the pastor on the basis of their expertise in matters related to accounting and finance, investment management, fundraising/development, budget, engineering, and law. The three-to-five-member finance council receives support and guidance from the diocesan Department of Finance.

The parish finance council and the parish pastoral council function interdependently; it is essential that they communicate with one another in furthering the parish mission. It is recommended that a member of the finance council attend pastoral council meetings to ensure continual sharing of information.

PARISH ROLES AND RESPONSIBILITIES

The following chart illustrates the distinct roles and responsibilities within the parish administrative and planning structures:

	Parish Administration	Pastoral Council	Finance Council
	(includes parochial vicar and parish staff)		
Pastor's Role	oversees daily operations	presides over	presides over
Membership	hired or appointed	selected through parish discernment process	appointed
Focus	day-to-day ministry	long-range pastoral planning	long-range financial planning
Areas of Responsibility	matters pertaining to a job description or specific area of parish life	matters pertaining to the life of the whole parish: essential elements	matters pertaining to budget, facilities, or development
Relationship to Pastoral Plan	assists as resource	develops, monitors, and evaluates plan	assists as resource
Relationship to Pastor	accountable to pastor	consultative to pastor	consultative to pastor
Method of Decision Making	by consensus when appropriate	by consensus	by consensus when appropriate

The Parish as One Body

All who share the ministry of leadership within the parish, therefore, have specific roles, tasks and functions. By working together for the realization of the parish mission, each group and all individuals play a significant part in accomplishing the goals and objectives of the pastoral plan.

St. Paul's analogy of the body is particularly appropriate here:

> If the whole body were an eye, where would the hearing be? If the whole body were hearing, where would the sense of smell be? But as it is, God placed the parts, each one of them, in the body as he intended.... The eye cannot say to the hand, "I do not need you," nor again the head to the feet, "I do not need you." Indeed, the parts of the body that seem to be weaker are all the more necessary.... Now you are Christ's body, and individually parts of it. (1 Cor. 12:17ff)

In this way, all members of the parish body work together to make its mission a reality. The clergy, pastoral council, parish staff, finance council, parish organizations, and all parishioners are vital parts of the whole. Together, they form the Body of Christ, and become the new wineskins into which the new wine of God's Word can be poured. In Christian unity, they discern the call of God to them in this particular time and place, and devote their individual and collective resources to bringing that mission to fulfillment.

"All members of the parish body... become the new wineskins into which the new wine of God's Word can be poured."

Relationship of the Parish to the Diocese

No parish exists in a vacuum of purpose or plans. In the Catholic tradition, the local church or diocese is a source of unity and a place where all pastoral life is supported and encouraged. The administration of each diocese may generate ways in which it establishes the relationship between central offices and individual parish pastoral councils. Such relationships would be dependent on the normal structures and communication patterns of the diocese. For example:

- Annually, the recorder may submit the names of the parish pastoral council members and the parish's pastoral plan to the diocesan office responsible for pastoral councils, which then reviews parish pastoral plans. This office may submit such reviews to its supervisor or to the vicar general, if so requested.
- Pastoral plans may be shared with the bishop, who refers to them at times of clergy transfers and appointments, and in preparation for any pastoral visits to the parish.
- The dean or vicar forane, when making parish visits, may use the parish pastoral plan to conduct the annual review of parish life with the parish pastoral council.

Other diocesan leadership bodies such as regional or vicariate councils and the diocesan pastoral council may refer to parish pastoral plans in their own visioning and planning efforts.

SELECTING NEW COUNCIL MEMBERS

THE PARISH COMMUNITY AND THE SELECTION PROCESS

Because the pastoral council is a visioning body, not a coordinating committee of ministries, eight to ten members are sufficient. In keeping with a pastoral—not a political—model, members of the council should be called forth from the community by a *selection* process rather than by election. The parish should use the following qualities as the selection criteria for those most gifted in the area of pastoral leadership.

Criteria for Selection

These basic criteria are considered necessary for a parishioner to be given selection consideration. The parishioner should

1. be a baptized, practicing Catholic.
2. have been a registered member of the parish for at least five years.
3. be a participant in the ongoing life of the parish, especially Sunday Eucharist.
4. be at least twenty-one years of age.

In addition, he or she should possess the following characteristics:

- a desire for spiritual growth in oneself and in the parish
- enthusiasm about the future directions of the parish
- willingness to listen, to speak honestly, and to work toward consensus
- the ability to inspire and empower others and to delegate
- flexibility and openness with people and ideas

Length of Service

It is recommended that the length of service for council members be no less than three years (excluding some need for a member to resign) and no more than nine. Continuity and stability without stagnation should be kept in mind when making decisions about length of service.

The Process of Selection

The process used for the identification and selection of members will vary from parish to parish, but should include some opportunity for the total parish to participate. This occurs by having parishioners identify potential parish leaders through communal prayer and a planned discernment process. The council, under the direction of the transition team, plans a process that includes:

- public and private prayer throughout the entire time of discerning new council members
- education and formation of parishioners on the role of the parish pastoral council
- explanation of particular qualities and gifts necessary for this leadership ministry
- an open invitation to parishioners to identify potential parish leaders: self and others
- an information session for those who have been identified
- a discernment session to select new members

Sample Pastoral Council Identification Form

Our parish needs Christian leadership to help make decisions about our pastoral life and growth. Please help identify persons in this faith community who could enable us to develop our sense of Evangelization, Worship, Word, Service, Community, Stewardship, and Leadership.

Leaders should have the following characteristics:

- a desire for spiritual growth in themselves and in the parish
- enthusiasm about the future directions of our parish
- willingness to listen, to speak honestly, and to work toward consensus
- the ability to inspire and empower others and to delegate
- flexibility and openness with people and ideas

In order to be considered for the ministry of parish leadership a parishioner must:

- be a baptized Catholic.
- have been be a registered member of our parish for at least five years.
- be a participant in the ongoing worship life of our parish, especially Sunday Eucharist.
- be at least twenty-one years old.

Since this is not a council of representatives, there is no need to consider representation of age groups. Nevertheless, we do need individuals whose maturity level allows them to be secure, confident, and comfortable in dealing with consensus and conflict. This type of maturity often comes with experience and age.

Please list the names of parishioners whom you identify as having the gifts for pastoral council leadership. These people will receive a call to inform them that they have been named and to ask them to participate in an information session. They will have the option to remain in the selection process or not.

IDENTIFICATION FORM FOR LEADERSHIP MINISTRY

I suggest that the following individuals be invited to consider leadership ministry through service on our parish pastoral council. I will continue to pray for the guidance of the Holy Spirit during the selection process.

______________________________ ______________________________

______________________________ ______________________________

______________________________ ______________________________

Thank you for your suggestions. Please pray for the selection of pastoral council leadership in our parish.

Information Session for Potential Council Members

The transition team assumes responsibility for organizing an information session to which all present and potential council members are invited. At the meeting:

- Plan to introduce all in the room. With more than fourteen persons, use an "ice breaker" which involves small groups and then the whole group. If a smaller group is gathered, simply do the exercise with the entire group.

- Provide a prayer seeking the assistance of the Holy Spirit in discernment and engaging all in faith sharing and petitions for the welfare of the parish.

- Share information on the REVISIONING THE PARISH PASTORAL COUNCIL process, including:
  - the basic difference between a parish council and a pastoral council
  - the seven elements of pastoral life with which the council concerns itself
  - decision-making by consensus
  - the planning process, both in general and in particular with regard to details of where the parish currently finds itself in the process (monitoring the plan, evaluation, assembly, revision of goals and objectives, or forming implementation groups)
  - roles of individuals and teams on council
  - details of the council's calendar, meeting times, annual retreat, workshops

End the session by announcing the date and time of the actual discernment (selection), asking all involved to pray for each other and for the work of the Holy Spirit in the final discernment.

Discernment for the Ministry of Leadership

Again, the transition team assumes responsibility for organizing the discernment process. They bring together present and potential council members, welcome them, and invite them into the prayer and discernment process. If short introductions are needed, they are made. Then a member of the team notes at the outset that the time needed for authentic discernment may exceed that allotted for a simpler meeting. Respectful listening and continuing prayer to the Holy Spirit mark the entire spirit of the gathering. *(A complete prayer service may be found in the "Prayer" section of Part I of this book.)*

The candidates are first asked to address several questions, without judgment, interrogation, or interruption by others in the room. Listed below are some suggested questions:

- For how long and in what ways have you been involved in our parish?
- What do you understand the work of this council to be?
- What one thing do you think would make the biggest difference in the spiritual life of our parish?
- What gifts do you possess which will enhance the work of the council?
- What drew you to offer your gifts to the ministry of leadership in our parish?
- What part of our mission statement is most challenging to you?

After the candidates have spoken, individuals may ask questions to help clarify what has been said. At this point, people may withdraw their names from consideration, although they should be invited to stay with the group through the rest of the process and to participate in the discernment.

Then the group begins the discernment for new members. Each person identifies several individuals whose gifts would bring a complementary presence to the present council. They then discuss the reasons for their choices.

If it appears that certain persons are clearly selected by the group, their names are listed. Continuing rounds of identifying persons with their gifts in relationship to the council are held until the full number of council members is selected.

If it appears that certain persons are discerned as equally possessing the gifts that are needed and the group cannot make a choice, after additional prayer, the member may be chosen in a caucus among those whose names are still in discernment.

Those selected sign their "Willingness to Serve" form. A final affirmation of consensus is voiced and a prayer of blessing and gratitude is offered. The names of those selected are announced to the parish as soon as possible.

SAMPLE OF "WILLINGNESS TO SERVE" FORM

I have studied the document, REVISIONING THE PARISH PASTORAL COUNCIL, and prayerfully considered the ministry of leadership. I believe I have the understanding and the needed gifts to commit myself to such ministry in our parish. I pledge to do my best to live up to the expectations involved in this ministry: to be a person of prayer, a good listener, enthusiastic about our future as a parish and concerned for the good of all. I agree to serve according to the requirements of Parish Pastoral Council membership.

Signature ______________________________ Date __________________

Suggested Timeline for the Pastoral Council Selection Process

Week 1 Begin publicity to entire parish on the WHY AND HOW of selection process.
Utilize bulletin, homily, posters, flyers, announcements, meetings with groups.
Include prayer at Sunday Eucharist: general intercessions, prayer cards.

Week 2 Continue publicity on the ROLE AND FUNCTION of the council.
Continue prayer.
Prepare forms for identifying potential candidates.
Develop details of information session for potential candidates.

Week 3 Continue publicity on the QUALITIES AND REQUIREMENTS of pastoral council members.
Continue prayer.
Finalize all details for process.

Week 4 Continue publicity at Masses and explain IDENTIFICATION FORMS.
Distribute Identification Forms; request their return by the following Sunday.
Continue prayer that parishioners with necessary gifts will be identified.

Week 5 Gather IDENTIFICATION FORMS.
Continue prayer for those who have been suggested.
Call all who have been identified to invite them to information session.

Week 6 Continue prayer for potential council members and for the Spirit's guidance in the discernment process.
Sponsor INFORMATION SESSION.

Week 7 ANNOUNCE NAMES of all who will be involved in the discernment.
Continue prayer for the working of the Spirit in the discernment process.
Conduct FORMAL DISCERNMENT PROCESS.
Have council members sign their "Willingness to Serve" form.

Week 8 Announce newly-selected council members.
Pray publicly for God's blessing on new council.

Week 9 Begin transition/orientation process.

MEETINGS

COUNCIL MEETINGS

When pastoral councils meet, the dynamics should be different from those of ordinary business meetings, given the purpose and responsibility of the group. Mindful of the mission to which they are called and the ministry of leadership which they exercise, members can nevertheless learn practical skills that make meetings productive as well as faithful to the purposes of the council.

Around the Council Meeting Table

Be willing to share your own ideas.

- Take the risk; your point of view is valuable.
- Speak up so others can hear you.
- Make eye contact.
- When speaking, use "I" instead of "we" or "they."
- Be aware of your body language.
- Stay with the issue being discussed.

Be willing to listen with an attempt to understand.

- Let others know if you can't hear them.
- Ask for clarification if you do not understand.
- Give everyone a chance to speak.
- Permit one person to speak at a time.
- Do not interrupt.

Value differences.

- Remember that each person has a part of the truth.
- Respect each person's contribution.
- Do not negate another's ideas or experiences.
- Appreciate and encourage different ideas, experiences, and opinions.

Be a person of faith.

- Strive to see Christ in each person at the meeting.
- Always keep the mission of Jesus, the Church, and your parish before you.
- Be open to the work of the Holy Spirit who may change everything around.

Those who are unable to learn from past meetings are condemned to repeat them.

MEETING BEHAVIOR AWARENESS SCALE

Consider these behaviors commonly observed at meetings. Realistically assess how often you presently exhibit each of them. Then indicate what you would like to change. Use the following scale:

1 — I never display this behavior.
2 — I sometimes display this behavior.
3 — I often display this behavior.

		Present Rating	*Desired Rating*
1.	I prepare for the meeting by studying the agenda.	_____	_____
2.	I carry out any assignment or role I have.	_____	_____
3.	I listen carefully to what others say.	_____	_____
4.	I allow people to express their ideas.	_____	_____
5.	I express my ideas on issues under discussion.	_____	_____
6.	I observe and respond to nonverbal cues from others.	_____	_____
7.	I help clarify the group's goals and questions.	_____	_____
8.	I contribute to discussions about priorities and decisions.	_____	_____
9.	I limit my remarks to the topic we are discussing.	_____	_____
10.	I encourage and seek out others' perspectives.	_____	_____
11.	I confidently express my own opinions.	_____	_____
12.	I help generate alternative solutions to issues.	_____	_____
13.	I summarize progress made on issues.	_____	_____
14.	I help resolve conflicts or disputes.	_____	_____
15.	I show respect to every person in the group.	_____	_____
16.	I discourage domination by individuals in the group.	_____	_____
17.	I block personal attacks and negative behavior.	_____	_____
18.	I refuse to engage in negative or hurtful attacks on others.	_____	_____
19.	I offer positive feedback to others.	_____	_____
20.	I encourage evaluation of our group's work.	_____	_____
21.	I arrive late for meetings or leave early.	_____	_____
22.	I keep quiet and limit my participation.	_____	_____
23.	I dominate meetings by talking a lot.	_____	_____
24.	I get off the topic and lose focus.	_____	_____
25.	I talk with others in side conversations.	_____	_____
26.	I belittle the contributions of others.	_____	_____
27.	I use excessive or inappropriate humor.	_____	_____
28.	I get hurt by what others say.	_____	_____
29.	I say what I think others want me to say.	_____	_____
30.	I talk with friends after the meeting about what I really think.	_____	_____

How to Conduct Meetings that Get You Where You're Going

1. **What's the Destination?**
    - Identify where you are going.
    - Plan how to get there.
    - Anticipate problems or roadblocks.
    - Evaluate at the end.

2. **What's the Purpose?**
    - A meeting to plan or decide
        - Invite all to be active participants.
        - Focus on the future, one idea at a time.
        - Brainstorm creatively.
        - Use consensus.
        - Make decision.
        - Be sure all can live with it.

    - A meeting to evaluate progress
        - Listen to those responsible for implementation.
        - Check all results against the mission.
        - Seek ways to improve.
        - Pray for openness to truth.
        - Consider using an outside facilitator.

3. **Who's Got the Map?**
    - Agenda team prepares timeline, process, topics.
    - Convener calls "travelers," prepares essential resources, materials, equipment.

4. **What Vehicles Will Get Us There?**
    - Convener prepares physical set-up (space, table arrangements, refreshments).
    - Recorder tracks progress on overhead projector or newsprint.

5. **Who Steers the Meeting?**
    - The facilitator has special responsibility for both content (what is to be done) and process (the dynamic for keeping the group functioning)
        - Facilitation guides a group to achieve its task. The facilitator is not an authority figure or a chairperson, but someone who makes meetings run smoothly.
        - The best facilitation looks easy but is hard work.

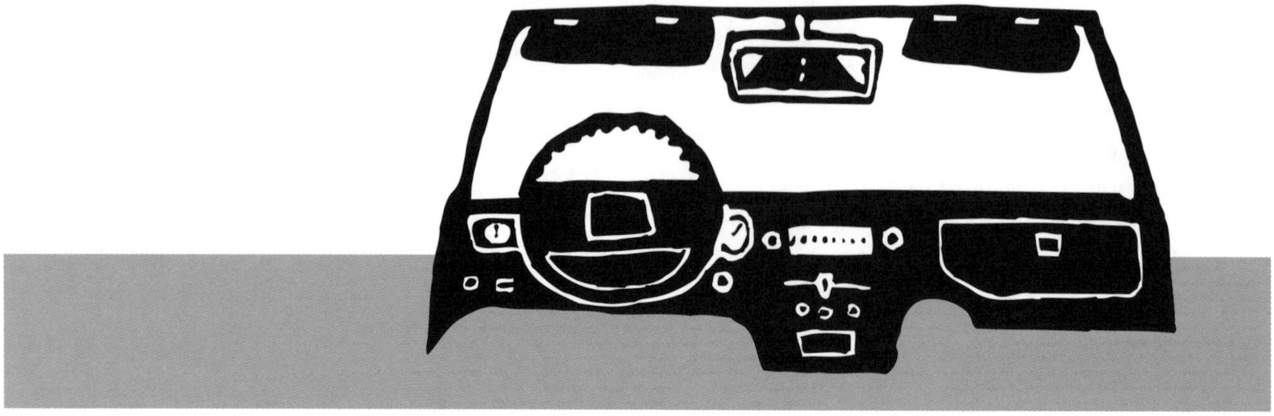

- Facilitator skills related to content
  - Introducing issues to the group
  - Giving information in the form of data, facts, opinions, ideas
  - Identifying what the council knows and does not know about the topic
  - Clarifying, answering, or referring questions; explaining, giving examples
  - Pointing out alternatives and options, and their implications
  - Keeping the group focused on the issues
  - Summarizing along the way and at the end of meetings

- Facilitator skills related to group process
  - Inviting persons to participate, to contribute ideas
  - Keeping dominating persons from excluding others
  - Maintaining a positive tone
  - Encouraging and giving feedback when members contribute their ideas or feelings
  - Mediating potential conflicts
  - Suggesting compromise or alternatives
  - Monitoring the climate; knowing when to call for a break, how to rephrase someone's comments, how to bring the conversation back to the topic

- Facilitator prepares and uses various tools for quick repairs along the way
  - ➤ For brainstorming
    - Solicit one idea from each participant.
    - Post each idea.
    - Consolidate similar ideas.
    - Select top three ideas.
    - Come to consensus on idea with strongest interest.

  - ➤ For starting discussion
    - Ask, "What is most interesting about this topic? How do you feel about this issue?"

- Have triads "buzz" to identify two or three facets of an issue.
- Propose the beginning of a thought for the group to complete: "What we need to learn is . . ." or "We could solve this problem if. . . ."

➤ For dealing with deadlocks
- Ask people to reverse positions and argue from the opposite side of the issue.
- Get the group to consider the consequences of each position.
- Encourage a caucus among proponents of each position.
- Call a break to allow for informal conversation; speak privately with the person causing the disruption.

➤ For moving past a slow issue
- Validate an unresolved issue by saving it on newsprint marked "parking lot."
- Return to the issue if time allows, (or)
- Refer the "parked" issue to a subgroup, (or)
- Determine to abandon the issue permanently.

6. Who's Along for the Ride?

- *Henrietta Hesitant*
  - You sense she disagrees but won't express an opinion. Ask, "Who hates this idea?" Prepare to hear negative comments once permission has been given for dissent.
  - She makes irrelevant comments without addressing the core issue. Say, "We'll note that comment on the newsprint. But now, what about . . . ?"

- *Willie Whiner*
  - He never has anything positive to say. Turn the negativity around. Ask, "How would you improve this? What could we do that would make it acceptable to you?"
  - Ask, "Is there anyone else who shares Willie's concerns?" If yes, open the discussion. If no, the whiner will see he's the only one who feels that way.

- *Rambling Rose*
  - She can't say anything in less than six paragraphs. Listen for a "hook" to take you back to the topic of the conversation. Say, "Speaking of . . . , could we return to our discussion on . . ."
  - At a pause, catch up to her ramblings and rephrase her basic opinion. "What I hear you saying is . . ." Thank her and move on.

- *Andy Anonymous*
  - He never has an opinion, but can always report what "they" think. Say firmly, "That's very interesting, but what is *your* position on the issue?"

- Ask, "To whom are you referring?" Or, "Are 'they' one or two people or a significant number?" Often it is one person who made a remark.

- *Rigid Brigid*
  - She won't listen, but keeps repeating her own idea over and over. Ask, "Is there anything new you'd like to add?"
  - Ask the group, "Are we pretty sure we know what Brigid thinks on this matter?"
  - Ask the recorder to be sure to note Brigid's opinion on the newsprint and quickly move on.

- *Coroner Mort*
  - He leaves meetings issuing grave post mortems. He passes on the bad news readily, and keeps the phone company happy. You probably can't change him.
  - Avoid entering into the negativity or getting caught up in post-meeting hand wringing. Say, "That wasn't my perception of the meeting. In fact, I thought . . ." (here insert some positive outcomes).

- *Whispering Winnie*
  - She carries on side conversations and distracts others. Don't embarrass her, but restate the last opinion and ask her, by name, for a comment.
  - A glance her way or a short pause in the meeting can get the message across.

- *Deferential Dave*
  - He defers to authority figures, usually to the pastor or facilitator. "Whatever Father says." Or "You're in charge here." Point out that everyone's ideas are needed.
  - State the issue from your point of view, then say, "Let's hear some other opinions." Ask Dave to respond.

- *Quincy Quiet*
  - Quincy doesn't talk; he may be bored, indifferent, feeling superior or insecure. Ask him gently and directly for an idea or opinion, allowing him to speak personally with you. Redirect his comments to the group or invite another member to enter the conversation.
  - Add a sincere compliment, "It's good to hear from you. Thanks for that idea."

- *Mollie Monopolizer*
  - She talks on and on, preventing others from getting into the conversation. When she pauses for a breath, say, "You've given us so much to think about. Let's hear what some other people are thinking." Redirect attention to the larger group.
  - If she does this frequently, request that everyone be heard before lengthy discussion begins. Or ask that everyone have the opportunity

to speak once before anyone speaks a second time. "Is there someone we haven't heard from yet?"

- *Toni the Tongue-tied*
  - Toni has the idea but can't express it in the right words. She needs help in articulating her point of view. Don't say, "I know what you mean . . ." but "Do you mean . . . ?"
  - Rephrase her comments, sticking as closely as possible to her actual words, but use good language and structure that makes sense. Verify with her that you have said what she really intends.

- *Fighting Frans*
  - Fran and Frannie disagree strongly and begin to get folks to take sides. Diffuse the dynamic by pointing out areas of agreement and minimizing areas of disagreement.
  - Find a third person (or be that person) who will introduce another position into the discussion. Create an option that respects both positions.
  - Say, "Let's discuss the merits of both of these positions and leave personalities out of it."

7. **How Was the Trip?**
   - Recap the purpose of the meeting.
   - Note your accomplishments.
   - Provide a summary, noting roles people played.
   - Project what will happen next.
   - Applaud everyone's efforts.
   - Debrief the meeting with the group. "How did we enjoy the ride?"

Suggested Planning Timeline for Council Meetings

Two Weeks Before the Meeting

1. Agenda team meets to plan agenda.
2. Recorder notifies spiritual formation team about special needs for prayer.
3. Recorder notifies convener about date and time, and any special set-up needs.

Ten Days Before the Meeting

4. Spiritual formation team meets to plan study, reflection, prayer.
5. Spiritual formation team notifies recorder about any readings or other preparation needed by council prior to meeting.

One Week Before the Meeting

6. Recorder sends out agenda to council members.
7. Spiritual formation team alerts convener to any special set-up needs.
8. Spiritual formation team contacts council members who will have roles in prayer, e.g., readers, cantor, prayer leader.
9. Facilitator reviews agenda and plans the flow of the meeting.

Three Days Before the Meeting

10. Convener calls each council member as a reminder about meeting, time and place.

(At Least One Hour Before the Meeting)

11. Convener makes meeting arrangements, setting up as needed. Considers space, seating, ambiance, refreshments, materials, equipment.

THE ACTUAL MEETING

One Week After the Meeting

13. Recorder distributes record of the meeting.

Annual Calendar

The annual calendar of the council relates to its pastoral planning cycle. More meetings may be necessary during the discernment or evaluation phases, for example, than during the implementation phase. This will vary from parish to parish and is at the discretion of the council and the pastor. A suggested calendar follows:

January: Evaluation
How did it go?

- Dialogue with implementation groups to evaluate each objective.

February–March: Review and Modify
Who are we?

- Mission Statement
- Goals
- New data
- Financial plan (with finance council)

April: Develop New Objectives
What do we want to do?

- Sponsor annual parish assembly.
- Share evaluations with parishioners.
- Brainstorm new objectives.

May–June: Empowerment
Who will implement the objectives?

- Publicize new objectives and invite parish involvement.
- Identify the appropriate groups to carry out each new objective.

July: Implementation Begins
How are we going to do it?

- Establish ad hoc implementation groups, budgets, action plans, and parish calendar.

August–December: Ongoing Council Life

- Participate in annual council retreat.
- Oversee groups and individuals who are implementing the objectives.
- Meet with Finance Council to review budget factors related to long-term pastoral plans.
- Attend to transitions of new pastor, staff, or pastoral council members.
- Host or attend regional or diocesan pastoral council gatherings.

CONCLUSION

In his October, 1995, visit to the United States, Pope John Paul II offered words of encouragement to all those who seek to spread the Gospel of Jesus Christ:

> The challenge of the great jubilee of the year 2000 is the new evangelization: a deepening of faith and a vigorous response to the Christian vocation to holiness and service. This is what the successor of Peter... urge[s] upon each one of you: the courage to bear witness to the Gospel of our redemption.[30]

This, indeed, is the essential mission of every parish and each person baptized in the name of Jesus Christ. By proclaiming the WORD, offering prayerful WORSHIP, forming a COMMUNITY of faith, placing ourselves at the SERVICE of others, exercising STEWARDSHIP over all God's gifts and a shared LEADERSHIP modeled on that of Christ himself, we fulfill the Church's essential mission of EVANGELIZATION.

Through the pastoral planning process, the pastor and pastoral council lead the parish in the discernment and expression of its mission. With the cooperation of the parochial vicars, parish staff, finance council, parish organizations and committees, and all parishioners, the parish pastoral council focuses the vision of the parish on the seven essential elements of parish life. A ministry of leadership that is rooted in the Spirit has the potential to continually pour the new wine of God's Word into the wineskin that is the parish. By revisioning the parish through the ministry of the parish pastoral council, the entire parish joins together in fulfilling its unique role within the local and universal Church.

NOTES

1. Austin Flannery, O.P., ed., "Decree on the Apostolate of Lay People," *Vatican Council II: The Conciliar and Post Conciliar Documents* (Boston: St. Paul Editions, 1998), 791-92.

2. Rev. William Dalton, "Parish Councils or Parish Pastoral Councils?" *Studia Canonica* 22 (1988): 169.

3. Flannery, "Dogmatic Constitution on the Church," 359.

4. Flannery, "Decree on the Apostolate of Lay People," 766.

5. Ibid., 777.

6. Ibid., 768.

7. Ibid., 781.

8. Walter Abbott and Joseph Gallagher, eds., Introduction to the "Decree on the Apostolate of the Laity," *The Documents of Vatican II* (New York: American Press, 1966), 486.

9. *Code of Canon Law,* Latin-English Edition (Canon Law Society of America, 1983). All subsequent references to canon law are from this edition.

10. National Conference of Catholic Bishops, *Communities of Salt and Light: Reflections on the Social Mission of the Parish* (National Conference of Catholic Bishops, 1993), 1.

11. Pope Paul VI, *On Evangelization in the Modern World,* December 8, 1975, #15.

12. Ibid., #14.

13. National Conference of Catholic Bishops, *Go and Make Disciples: A National Plan and Strategy for Catholic Evangelization in the United States* (National Conference of Catholic Bishops, 1992), 7-8.

14. Flannery, "Constitution on the Sacred Liturgy," Introduction, 2.

15. Flannery, "Decree on the Apostolate of Lay People," 777.

16. United States Catholic Conference, *The Catechism of the Catholic Church* (United States Catholic Conference, 1994), Prologue, 4, 6.

17. Flannery, "Dogmatic Constitution on the Church," 352.

18. Ibid., 364.

19. Ibid.

20. Cf. Matthew 5:3-12; 9:35-38; 15:29-31; Mark 6:7-13; Luke 6:17-22 and 27-42; 10:29-37; 22:24-30; John 13:1-17 and 34-35.

21. *Communities of Salt and Light,* 1, 3.

22. Ibid., 12-13.

23. National Conference of Catholic Bishops, *Stewardship: A Disciple's Response* (National Conference of Catholic Bishops, 1992).

24. Flannery, "Constitution on the Sacred Liturgy," 5.

25. *The Catechism of the Catholic Church,* 338.

26. Flannery, "Decree on the Ministry and Life of Priests," 863 ff.

27. Flannery, "Dogmatic Constitution on the Church," 395.

28. *Code of Canon Law,* canon 536.

29. Joseph A. Janicki, "Commentary on Parish Councils—Canon 536," in *The Code of Canon Law: A Text and Commentary,* ed. James A. Coriden, Thomas J. Green, Donald E. Heintschel (New York: Paulist Press, 1985), 431.

30. Pope John Paul II, Homily at the Mass at Camden Yards Stadium, Baltimore, Md., October 8, 1995. *Origins* 25 (October 19, 1995): 18.

RESOURCES

EVANGELIZATION RESOURCES

On Evangelization in the Modern World (*Evangelii Nuntiandi*).
Pope Paul VI. USCC Publishing Services, 1975.
The foundational document on modern Catholic evangelization, "the essential mission of the Church."

The Mission of the Redeemer (*Redemptoris Missio*).
Pope John Paul II. USCC Publishing Services, 1991.
A new call to commit the Church to the evangelization of the world, emphasizing the centrality of Jesus Christ and the Church's inescapable role in proclaiming him.

Go and Make Disciples: A National Plan and Strategy for Catholic Evangelization in the United States.
National Conference of Catholic Bishops. USCC Publishing Services, 1992.
A spiritual vision of evangelization, followed by three goals for our Church and numerous strategies for achieving them. A "brainstorming" document useful to any interested group (e.g., parish staff, parish pastoral council, parish organizations).

Commentary and Planning Guide for Go and Make Disciples.
Paulist National Catholic Evangelization Assoc., Washington, D.C. (1-800-237-5515).

Text, Study Guide, and Implementation Process for Go and Make Disciples.
National Council for Catholic Evangelization, Manassas, Va. (1-800-786-NCCE).

Notes:

USCC Publishing issues a catalog of official church documents. For a catalog or to place an order, call 1-800-235-8722.

The Paulist National Catholic Evangelization Association, Washington, D.C. (1-800-237-5515) distributes an extensive line of resources in the area of evangelization.

WORSHIP RESOURCES

Major sources for good quality books on the liturgy:

Liturgy Training Publications (LTP)
(Archdiocese of Chicago)
1800 N. Hermitage Avenue
Chicago, Ill. 60622-1101
1-800-933-1800

The Liturgical Press (LP)
Saint John's Abbey
Collegeville, Minn. 56321-7500
612-363-2213

The Pastoral Press (PP)
225 Sheridan Street, NW
Washington, D.C. 20011-1492
202-723-1254

USCC Publishing Services
3211 Fourth Street, NE
Washington, D.C. 20017
1-800-235-8722

WORD RESOURCES

General Directory for Catechesis 1997
Published in the United States by the United States Catholic Conference, 1998.
Most recent universal guidelines and directives for catechesis.

Rite of Christian Initiation of Adults
1988 edition. An absolutely indispensable book of the rite itself. Available from various publishers in both hardback and softcover format. This and other RCIA printed materials are produced by:
Liturgy Training Publications
800 N. Hermitage Avenue
Chicago, IL 60622-1101
1-800-933-1800

On Catechesis in Our Time (*Catechesi Tradendae*)
Pope John Paul II: 1979. Printed in the U.S. by the Daughters of St. Paul.

To Teach As Jesus Did: A Pastoral Message on Catholic Education
National Conference of Catholic Bishops: 1972.
Publications Office, United States Catholic Conference.

Sharing the Light of Faith.
National Catechetical Directory for Catholics of the United States.
United States Catholic Conference, Department of Education, 1979.

The Catechism of the Catholic Church
United States Catholic Conference, 1994.

COMMUNITY RESOURCES

Dogmatic Constitution on the Church
Pastoral Constitution on the Church in the Modern World
In *Vatican Council II, Constitutions, Decrees, Declarations,* Austin Flannery, O.P., General Editor.
Northport, N.Y.: Costello Publishing Company, 1996.

Code, Community, Ministry
ed. Edward G. Pfnausch.
Canon Law Society of America, 1992.

The National Catholic Convening on Aging,
Catholic Charities USA.
Alexandria, Va.,1994.

On the Family, Apostolic Exhortation of John Paul II
Washington, D.C.: USCC, 1981.

A Family Perspective in Church and Society: A Manual for All Pastoral Leaders
Washington, D.C.: USCC, 1988.

Families at the Center: A Handbook for Parish Ministry with a Family Perspective
Washington, D.C.: USCC, 1988.

Putting Children and Families First: A Challenge for Our Church, Nation, and World
Washington, D.C.: USCC: 1991.

Pastoral Statement of US Catholic Bishops on Persons with Disabilities
Washington, D.C.: National Conference of Catholic Bishops (NCCB), 1978. (Revised 1989).

Guidelines for Celebration of the Sacraments with People with Disabilities
National Conference of Catholic Bishops (NCCB)
Washington, D.C.: USCC, 1995.

National Catholic Office for Persons with Disabilities
P.O. Box 29113, Washington, D.C. 20017.
202/529-4678.

NOTE:

To order USCC publications, contact the USCC Office for Publishing and Promotion Services, 3211 Fourth Street, NE, Washington, D.C. 20017-1194; Telephone-800-235-8722.

SERVICE RESOURCES

Communities of Salt & Light: Reflections on the Social Mission of the Parish
National Conference of Catholic Bishops, 1993.

Some Specific Topics of Catholic Social Teaching (NCCB)

- The Rights of Workers and the Dignity of Work
- Economic Justice for All
- The Right to Own Property
- Responsibility to Participate in Society
- Advocating for the Poor and Vulnerable
- The Challenge of Peace
- Abortion & Euthanasia
- Pastoral Plan for Pro-Life Activities
- Family Unity
- The Ecology
- The Rights of Women
- Racial Equality
- Rights of People with Disabilities

STEWARDSHIP RESOURCES

Stewardship: A Disciple's Response
National Conference of Catholic Bishops, 1993.
Jesus calls us, as his disciples, to a new way of life—the Christian way of life—of which stewardship is a part. As Christian stewards, we receive

God's gifts gratefully, cultivate them responsibly, share them lovingly in justice with others, and return them with increase to the Lord.

To Be a Christian Steward
National Conference of Catholic Bishops, 1993.
Summary of bishops' statement on stewardship. Designed and priced for wide distribution.

LEADERSHIP RESOURCES

The Parish—A People, A Mission, A Structure
National Conference of Catholic Bishops, Washington, D.C., 1981.

Vatican Council II, Constitutions, Decrees, Declarations
Austin Flannery, O.P. General Editor.
Northport, N.Y.: Costello Publishing Company, 1996.

New Parish Ministers: Laity and Religious on Parish Staffs
Philip J. Murnion.
National Pastoral Life Center, 1992.

DIOCESAN SERVICES

(Keep a list of diocesan offices and phone numbers here.)